I0453244

THE PSYCHOLOGY OF TEMPTATION

THE INVISIBLE GAME OF THE FALL

ERIC ALBERTO

The Psychology of Temptation
The Invisible Game of the Fall

© 2025 by Eric Alberto

All rights reserved. No part of this publication may be reproduced, distributed, or transmitted in any form or by any means, including photocopying, recording, or other electronic or mechanical methods, without the prior written permission of the publisher, except in the case of brief quotations used in reviews, articles, or critical references.

ISBN: 979-8-9999834-1-1

Cover Design: Eric Alberto

Design and Layout: Marcus Munhoz

Manuscript preparation and editing: Eric Alberto

First Edition — August 2025

Printed in the United States of America

Cross Publishing

www.editoracross.com

TABLE OF CONTENTS

INTRODUCTION

The history of humanity is, at its core, a history of temptation.

From Eden to the digital age, from David's palace to the luxurious headquarters of major corporations, from Judas's coins to the moral concessions we make in front of a screen; the pattern repeats itself.

But what if temptation were not merely a spiritual issue or a test of character? What if it were also a psychological and neurological mechanism, designed to lead us into a fall before we even notice the first step?

Just last week, we witnessed a simple scene at home. Our daughter, Rachel Skye, just four years old, received a lollipop on a Monday. My wife told her she could only eat it on Saturday. Throughout the entire week, the lollipop was within reach. Every day, she asked, "Is it Saturday yet, Mommy?"

On Thursday, my wife noticed in the car's rearview mirror that Rachel was holding the lollipop close to her mouth. Before any reprimand, she said, "I'm just smelling it, Mommy."

She didn't give in. Even without fully understanding, she showed that it's possible to resist; that desire doesn't have to control us.

This kind of situation illustrates how temptation challenges us to resist instant pleasure. It is not an unbeatable monster. It can be controlled. It can be defeated by those who choose to delay momentary pleasure in order to achieve something greater.

Now, take a look at your own life. Every day, you face invisible battles:

- The glance that challenges your faithfulness.

- The opportunity for quick profit that demands you give up values you swore to uphold.

- The unguarded word that, if spoken, could destroy years of trust.

The real question is: Are you waiting for the right reward, or are you surrendering to immediate pleasure?

Throughout history, kings, warriors, and nations have been defeated not by armies, but by temptations that arrived like a whisper. From Eden to the wilderness, from Eve to Jesus, we see a single storyline: some give in, others overcome. And the difference lies in mastering the heart and mind.

Today, temptation is no longer confined to gardens or deserts. It moves silently, almost imperceptibly, like a shadow that learns your rhythm, breathes your air, and waits for your distraction. It doesn't need to shout. It acts when you don't realize you're being watched.

And yet, we keep falling.

Why?

Because temptation strikes at the weakest zone of our mind: the craving for instant gratification. Neuroscience shows that it activates the same circuits as addiction, fueling our impulsiveness. The enemy doesn't have to push us. He only needs to pull the right triggers.

For too long, we've heard simplistic answers:

"Just have more willpower."

But what if your willpower runs out?

"Just ignore it."

But ignoring something that's already invaded your thoughts is pointless.

"Just pray and fast."

That is essential, but God also gave us intelligence and strategy to resist.

The truth is, temptation doesn't begin at the moment of decision.

It infiltrates your habits, your repetitive thoughts, the patterns you cultivate daily.

This book is not a moralistic sermon about right and wrong.

It is a strategic roadmap to show you:

- How your brain builds desires and how to reprogram them before it's too late.

- Why small compromises are more dangerous than major falls.

- How certain temptations disguise themselves as opportunities and can ruin your life.

- How to identify and dismantle emotional triggers.

- How to unite biblical principles with scientific discoveries to shield your mind and heart.

You won't just understand temptation. You will learn to defeat it.

And now, you have two choices:

Close this book and keep ignoring the patterns that push you toward the fall.

Or keep reading and take control of your own mind; before it's too late.

If you choose the second option, get ready. You may discover that your downfalls were never just personal weaknesses, but the result of a calculated strategy to bring you down. The only way to win a war is to understand the enemy's tactics.

And now, you are about to see how he truly operates.

WELCOME TO THE
PSYCHOLOGY OF
TEMPTATION.

THE MECHANISM OF TEMPTATION:

HOW THE SERPENT BUILDS ITS TRAPS

"A traveler walks through a dense forest. The silence is absolute, the path seems safe. But beneath the dry leaves, something invisible waits. A single misstep. A snap. The ground gives way, and in seconds, the trap closes around him. Temptation never presents itself as an obvious threat. It simply creates the perfect environment and waits for the victim to complete the journey toward the fall."

You don't fall suddenly. No one falls suddenly. Before every downfall, there is always a whisper. A convincing argument. A plausible excuse. A silent desire. That is how it begins. Not with the sin itself, but with the permission to think about it.

Temptation does not arrive shouting. It whispers. It does not force, it invites. It does not push, it suggests. It presents itself as a logical relief, an answer to your exhaustion, a solution for a real pain. But it always hides the cost. The greatest danger of temptation is not in what it shows, but in what it deliberately conceals.

We live in a new Eden. The garden is now digital, and the forbidden tree is in your pocket. The serpent does not speak with a human voice. It manifests through notifications. Its whispers are algorithms. With every swipe of your finger, an intelligent system maps your desires, learns your triggers, and identifies your impulses. Then, it offers exactly what will feed your appetite and weaken your self-control.

Imagine John, a disciplined Christian. He wakes up with the desire to pray and read the Word, but first decides to take just a quick look at his phone. Forty-seven minutes later, he realizes he has been pulled into stories, videos, and posts that stirred emotions, memories, and dormant desires. The serpent no longer needs to convince. It only needs to notify.

This is the new Eden. The garden is digital. The forbidden tree is just one tap away.

THE THREE-STAGE CYCLE OF TEMPTATION

Since Genesis, the script of temptation has never changed. It is subtle but strategically crafted. First comes suggestion, then rationalization, and finally the activated desire. Three acts, one tragic ending.

It all begins with doubt. The suggestion is not a direct affront but an almost harmless insinuation: Did God really say that? This question, as old as Eden itself, does not seek clarity, it seeks to erode conviction. A seemingly neutral thought sneaks in, a harmless curiosity becomes the entry point for an internal crisis. Without realizing it, the mind starts paving the road to a fall.

Next comes rationalization. The serpent's voice now echoes like your own conscience: You will certainly not die. The error begins to seem acceptable. The mind justifies. The conscience negotiates. What was non-negotiable yesterday now seems understandable today. Absolute truths begin to appear flexible. Morality bends to desire, and sin is repackaged with the makeup of logic. Truth, when relativized, loses its power to convenience.

When the heart has already been convinced, desire is activated: The tree was pleasing to the eyes. Now, thought turns into will, and will turns into action. Resistance, emptied by the previous stages, collapses without direct confrontation. Temptation achieves its goal. The fall is not a sudden stumble, it is the final destination of a path that began with a single thought.

This same script was used against Jesus in the wilderness. The suggestion came in the form of need: Turn these stones into bread. The rationalization hid behind a spiritual promise: Throw yourself down, and the angels will catch you. The final desire offered power and glory: I will give you all the kingdoms of the world.

But unlike Eve, Jesus did not enter into dialogue. He did not ponder. He cut the cycle at the very first thought, using the only weapon capable of breaking mental seduction: the truth. Temptation only becomes uncontrollable when it is welcomed as a possibility. Jesus showed that it can be defeated before it even turns into desire.

THE REWARD EXPERIMENT: HOW TEMPTATION TRAPS THE MIND

In 1954, James Olds and Peter Milner implanted electrodes in rats, connecting them to the area of the brain responsible for pleasure. The rats pressed the button that activated this region repeatedly, until they died of exhaustion, ignoring food, water, and rest. They were not destroyed by hunger or pain, but by the illusion of continuous pleasure.

Today, we live through a similar experiment, but on a global scale. The button has changed shape, it is now called Instagram, YouTube, TikTok, pornography, compulsive consumption, and more. The mechanism is the same. Highly addictive stimuli hijack the brain's reward system. Dopamine, the pleasure neurotransmitter, is captured by algorithms that study our habits, impulses, and triggers. Temptation disguises itself as entertainment, opportunity, or even as something you deserve. But its goal remains the same: to weaken control and promote dependency.

And the most alarming part? Pleasure has become a prison. What seemed harmless, a click, a curiosity, a distraction, turns into an emotional chain that enslaves. Temptation does not destroy us all at once. It numbs us. It intoxicates us slowly, until destruction feels comfortable, until ruin looks like routine.

The fall never happens suddenly. It is built in silence. First, we lose vigilance. Then, we tolerate the thought. Next, we give voice to the desire. Finally, the action feels inevitable, as if the mistake were just the natural consequence of everything we have already allowed inside.

Eve did not fall when she bit the fruit. She fell when she listened to the serpent without rebuking it. The battle was lost in the mind. The battlefield is mental, and surrender begins the moment we stop resisting the wrong argument. The serpent does not need to scream. It just needs to be heard.

This is where many stumble. Not every thought deserves hospitality. Not every idea that knocks on the door should be let in. Some come looking polite, but carry venom hidden in the subtext. Temptation rarely shows up with a shocking proposal. It starts with a subtle, dangerous doubt: Is it really that wrong?

The phrases that ruin a life are usually gentle: It is just for today. God will understand. I will ask for forgiveness later. Everyone does it. These are not just excuses. They are mental codes that reprogram the conscience. They are traps disguised as logic. The enemy does not need to shock you with sin, he only needs to convince you that it is not that serious.

When the mind begins negotiating with temptation, the heart is already losing its strength. Sin does not enter through the door of will, it slips through the window of imagination. That is why resisting means breaking the cycle before it blooms. It is about treating every thought like a seed. Seeds do not seem dangerous, but if ignored, they take root. And once rooted, they become trees. Trees will inevitably bear fruit. Sin does not start with weakness. It starts with the delay to confront the wrong thought.

HOW TO REPROGRAM THE MIND TO RESIST

Resisting temptation is not just a momentary reaction. It is a daily, intentional construction, like the silent training of a soldier preparing long before the war begins. A mind that resists is one that has been molded not in the heat of battle, but in the backstage of routine, in the invisible details of daily life.

Recognize the triggers with humility. No temptation comes from nowhere. It always carries an emotional address, an origin. It might be accumulated fatigue, the loneliness of an evening, or scrolling through social media on a low day. Identify the places, the people, the feelings, and the times that set off the red alert. Mapping temptation is the first step to defeating it. Every temptation has a path. And every path can be blocked if you know where it begins.

Get out of the danger zone. No one sinks in quicksand unless they step into it. There is no true resistance if you insist on staying surrounded by what weakens you. Sometimes, the problem is not the strength of temptation, but your insistence on staying where it is strongest. Cut access points. Eliminate shortcuts. Silence voices. Whoever escapes the environment of the fall has already won half the battle. Avoid the abyss, not because you are weak, but because you know how much your soul is worth.

Respond with truth. Jesus did not defeat Satan in the wilderness with motivational phrases. He defeated him with the Word. Lies are not fought with emotion, they are fought with conviction. Memorize Scripture. Meditate on it. Declare it. Truth is the only sword sharp enough to cut temptation at its root before it flowers. The devil does not fear those who merely know the truth, he flees from those who live by it.

Train self-control in daily life. Self-control is not born on the battlefield. It is forged in the kitchen, in the bedroom, in traffic, on the newsfeed. In the quiet, small decisions of everyday life. Saying no to the third piece of cake. Saying no to that unnecessary click. Saying no when no one is watching. Each quiet no is a brick in the wall of resistance. Temptation only wins against those who neglect the building of self-control.

Replace the stimulus, not just the act. Temptation is powerful because it offers pleasure. The mistake is believing that the answer is only to deny it. It is not enough to say no. You must say yes to something greater. Walk. Pray. Read. Talk to someone. Replace the stimulus with the habit that should be there in the first place. What is not filled with purpose will inevitably be occupied by impulses.

Surround yourself with people who inspire you to resist. No one wins alone. Temptation grows in silence. Victory blooms in community. Have people around you who speak truth when you are blind. People who push you toward God when your instinct is to run. Environment shapes behavior. And community can be your shield in moments of vulnerability. Walk with the wise, and you will learn to wait. Walk with the reckless, and you will fall.

Reprogramming the mind is like restoring a devastated garden. It requires pulling weeds, watering with purpose, protecting from shadows, and nourishing with the light of the Word. A trained mind does not win because temptation disappears. It wins because, even before temptation arrives, it has already decided who it belongs to.

Chapter 2

THE "JUST ONCE" EFFECT:

WHY SMALL SLIPS CREATE BIG DISASTERS

"A single strand of hair weighs nothing, but tie a hundred of them together and you have a rope strong enough to hold someone. Small slips become invisible chains."

Before a marriage is destroyed, there was a harmless-looking text message. Before a business owner was caught in a fraud scheme, there was a small financial adjustment justified by a momentary need. Before an addiction took over a life, there was a moment of "just once." The problem is not the isolated mistake, but the illusion that it is harmless. Small acts, when repeated, build the staircase that leads to moral collapse.

These small concessions create an internal pattern. The next wrong choice becomes easier. After a while, these deviations are no longer perceived as deviations, but as a new normal. This is not only a moral or spiritual phenomenon. Neuroscience proves that repetitive patterns shape the brain, turning occasional mistakes into automatic routines. By the time the person realizes it, they are already trapped in a cycle that feels impossible to break.

In a fast-paced consumer culture, like on Black Friday, "just this time" is pushed by notifications, flash sales, and emotional triggers. One click turns into compulsion. The same mechanism operates in spiritual temptation: error is disguised as opportunity, and the brain learns to desire what it once resisted. The real challenge is not only avoiding the big fall, but recognizing the small missteps that, when added together, pave the road to the abyss.

HOW THE MIND DECEIVES ITSELF: THE MENTAL SCRIPT OF JUSTIFICATION

This modern story only confirms what has always been true: sin is rarely a leap. It is a subtle construction. Moral collapse is born out of small ethical shifts that quietly pile up. Picture the brain as an untouched field of grass. Each choice is like carving a trail through it. The more you walk that trail, the clearer and easier it becomes to travel. The mind automates the path, and the habit takes the wheel.

This process has a name: **neuroplasticity**. The brain is moldable. Every repetition reinforces a neural connection. The more you walk that path, the more automatic your response becomes. Sin stops feeling like a conscious transgression and starts to feel like a neurologically accepted routine. Not because you are evil, but because your brain has been programmed that way.

Charles Duhigg describes this pattern as the habit loop: **cue, routine, reward**. The stress of the day drives you to scroll your social media feed, which gives relief and a dopamine hit. Over time, the brain associates relief with the click, not with truth. The result? A brain trained to seek comfort in behavior, even when that behavior contradicts your faith.

But there is an even more dangerous phenomenon: **cognitive dissonance**. When we act against what we believe, the brain enters into conflict. Instead of correcting the behavior, it adjusts the belief to relieve the discomfort. "Everyone does this." "God understands my weaknesses." Truth is not abandoned, it is rebranded. And sin becomes domesticated.

There is a deceptive sense of peace that comes with the first slips: the false feeling that "everything is still under control." You don't feel guilty because you are still praying. Still reading the Bible. Still attending church. But this is the enemy's most subtle trap: making you confuse attendance with alignment, frequency with faithfulness.

Without realizing it, you walk on what looks like firm ground but is actually ethical quicksand. At first, it feels solid, but with every concession, the ground becomes more unstable. First, your heel sinks. Then your knee. Finally, your entire body is swallowed. And the cruelest part? You only realize the danger when your spiritual oxygen is running out.

THE "JUST ONCE" TRAP

"Just once" is the most dangerous disguise of the fall. It smiles, seems harmless, and offers relief. But behind that smile is a sentence: "You can stop whenever you want." And it is precisely because you believe that, you continue. "Nobody saw." "It didn't hurt anyone." These are just the logical shells of a subtle poison. When Satan hears someone say, "It was just a thought," he doesn't need to push or scream. He just waits. Because he knows that from this point on, it is only a matter of time.

Some sink all at once. Others slowly get used to the depth. The enemy does not rush those who are already walking in the wrong direction. He simply stretches the silence between the first step and the last breath.

Samson did not lose his strength overnight. He gave it away little by little, as someone who sells a treasure in installments for convenience. His strength was not just physical, it was symbolic: it represented the commitment of his covenant with God. But Samson began to treat what was sacred as if it were common. He played with vows that were meant to be non-negotiable. He involved himself with women who embodied divine warnings. Delilah was not the first trap—she was simply the final chapter of a series of concessions. His fall was not sudden; it was cumulative. Samson did not fall from one blow. He fell through repetition.

Judas did not start out as a traitor. He was a disciple, chosen by Jesus, present during miracles, sermons, and private conversations. But his love for money revealed a crack he never dealt with. As treasurer, he began diverting small amounts. He justified it. No one noticed. Over time, even he stopped noticing. His heart, once molded by the Master's voice, was being trained by the sound of coins. When Satan saw that ground, he didn't need to force anything. He just whispered an offer. The rest was a consequence.

David didn't fall into adultery as someone who slips on a wet floor. It was wartime, but he chose to remain in the palace. The place he should have been was the battle-field, leading men, fulfilling his calling. But he chose com-fort. And comfort not only removed him from the war, but also exposed his soul to boredom. Boredom opened the door to the gaze. The gaze turned into desire. Desire turned into action. And action, into tragedy. Each step was a rationalized decision. He did not fall off a cliff. He walked down a staircase, convinced he could climb back up whenever he wanted.

HOW TO BREAK THIS CYCLE BEFORE IT IS TOO LATE

Recognize the start before mourning the end. A fall never begins at the abyss. It begins with an unchal-lenged thought, with silent permission, with a justifica-tion that sounds logical. Sin doesn't shout, it whispers. That is why the most effective vigilance does not happen at the moment of the fall, but at the door of entry. True spiritual warfare happens in the backstage of the mind, long before any outward exposure. Ask yourself: "What am I letting grow inside me while it still looks harmless?"

Environments shape decisions. Expose yourself to what strengthens you, and flee from what weakens you. Spiritual strength is not measured only by resistance but by the wisdom of not putting yourself to the test unneces-sarily. Many people stumble not because they were weak, but because they were in the wrong place, with the wrong people, at the wrong time. Environments are incubators of habits. Do not test your faith in places where your flesh feels at home. If you already know what weakens you, respect that internal warning as God's alarm. Ignored temptation turns into a prison waiting to happen.

Break the repetition with concrete actions. No pattern breaks by itself. Willpower without action is just theory. If you want to break the cycle, replace the automatic with intentional behavior. Replace the repetitive gesture with a ritual of truth. Instead of hiding in silence, seek refuge in a conversation with someone mature. Instead of giving in to the anxious click, anchor your mind with an eternal truth. The brain does not respond to guilt. It responds to repetition.

Saying "no" is building identity. Every time you say "no" to something you want but know violates your essence, you are saying "yes" to the purpose you were called to live. Holiness is built in intimacy, in the backstage of daily life, in decisions that no one applauds, but heaven records. You are not simply depriving yourself of something. You are strengthening yourself for something greater.

Understand that every "yes" has a price. Saying "yes" to error is signing the contract of self-sabotage. No wrong choice is neutral. Every "yes" to what enslaves rewrites your story and pushes your soul further from its purpose. But it is equally true that every conscious "no" has the power to redirect your history. Your life is not being shaped by big events, but by small decisions you repeat with consistency.

Restoration starts now. The mind programmed for error can be restored by truth. But restoration starts now. Do not wait for the next service, the next retreat, or the "last mistake" to start over. A restart does not happen on the stage. It begins with the thought you choose to rebuke, the click you choose to avoid, the conversation you choose not to start. Grace is available now. And the now is the most strategic place to defeat the "just one more time" before it becomes "I can't stop anymore."

HOW SATAN USES IMPULSIVENESS AGAINST YOU

"A thirsty traveler sees a river in the distance. His steps quicken, and his need speaks louder than reason. He ignores the warning signs around him, jumps into the water without noticing it is a trap. The current grabs him, and before he realizes it, he is being dragged to a destination he never chose."

This is how the temptation of haste works: it looks like instant relief, but it can turn into a prison.

Hunger distorts judgment. When a need becomes urgent, the brain switches to survival mode. In that state, immediate relief becomes the priority, and consequences are ignored. Wisdom gives way to impulse. But hunger is not just for food. There is hunger for recognition, stability, affection, control. And when that hunger runs deep, any proposal feels like the answer, even if it carries the taste of eternal loss.

Claudio was a Christian, father of two children, and the sales manager of a promising company. After months of piled-up bills and family tension, he received an unexpected proposal: to sell his share of the company for a fair price, paid in cash, without bureaucracy. The urgency seemed justified. The relief felt like an answered prayer. But along with the proposal came the ticking clock of anxiety.

"What good is it to wait? I need to solve this now."

He signed the contract without seeking counsel, without praying, just trying to silence the noise inside him. Two months later, the company was acquired by an international group. The partners who stayed became prosperous. Claudio was left with the immediate payout but with the emptiness of having traded purpose for

"Look, I am about to die. What good is the birthright to me?"
(Genesis 25:32)

haste. He did not fall because of greed. He stumbled because of urgency. His mistake was not desiring relief, but failing to discern the cost of rushing.

According to the book of Genesis, Esau was not dying. He was hungry. But hunger mixed with haste turns exaggeration into truth. He didn't trade just a plate of food. He sacrificed a legacy. He exchanged the invisible for the tangible. The eternal for the immediate. What should have been guarded was trivialized. What should have been celebrated was discarded.

This emotional urgency is alive today. It shows up in proposals that seem too good to wait for. In saying "yes" to a job offer that pays more but forces you to sacrifice time with family, your health, or your integrity. In promises of quick wealth, where profit is guaranteed even before effort is made. In emotional relationships that inflate the ego but drain the soul. In projects that seem like blessings but trample on your peace. In advice that sounds reasonable but silences the time of prayer.

Urgency does not knock on the door screaming. It arrives disguised as opportunity. And when you realize it, you have already crossed the line of prudence. Not every open door is from God. Not every countdown is a divine sign. The rhythm of the soul is slower than the rhythm of the world. Those who rush too much may outrun the promise.

THE NEUROSCIENCE OF HASTE

Have you noticed how everything around you demands immediate responses? One click, one delivery, one instant reply. We live under the rule of notifications and tight deadlines, as if now were the only legitimate time to act. But the human brain was not designed for complex decisions at such a fast pace. Under pressure, it activates its quick-response system, which operates based on instinct, not reflection. This mechanism, useful in survival situations, becomes a silent saboteur when choices require wisdom.

Under constant stress, the brain stays in a continuous alert state. Over time, it stops analyzing and starts reacting. And the most concerning part is that this system does not differentiate between a real threat and emotional pressure. The proposal with a short deadline, the decision made in the heat of the moment, the impulse to solve everything immediately, are all interpreted as risk situations. The prefrontal cortex, responsible for moral judgment and planning, reduces its activity. The result is a mind that acts on impulse, not conviction. Haste becomes the rule, not the exception.

On top of this, the brain's reward system comes into play. Dopamine, the neurotransmitter responsible for pleasure and motivation, is not released only when a goal is achieved but also when there is the expectation of relief. Just the thought of solving a problem triggers a chemical sense of pleasure, even if the solution is rushed, fragile, or destructive. The body feels relief before the decision is even made. And when this cycle repeats, the brain begins to favor shortcuts over real paths. Quick answers over deep reflections.

The brain learns through repetition. When you frequently choose the fastest, easiest, or most impulsive route, it recognizes this as the preferred path. This forms neural trails that condition behavior to avoid any kind of waiting. This phenomenon, known as automatism, reinforces immediacy as a natural reflex. The more these routes are reinforced, the weaker the muscle of patience becomes. The result is a brain trained to react, not to reflect. A mind that sees waiting as a loss and speed as a virtue.

HOW TO DEVELOP SELF-CONTROL AND MASTER HASTE

Train yourself to wait before waiting becomes your only option. Do not wait to be tested before learning how to resist. Patience is not born on the battlefield but in the field of daily training. Start small. Hold back from giving an impulsive answer. Pause before clicking "buy." Pray longer before saying "yes." Waiting is not just a mental exercise, it is the strengthening of the soul. Those who discipline themselves in calm moments are better prepared to stand firm in the storm.

Question all urgency, even when it seems legitimate. Haste often wears the mask of responsibility, but beneath it may live anxiety, fear, or insecurity. Every decision needs to pass through a spiritual filter: Am I acting out of conviction or fear of losing something? What is born of faith brings peace with it. What is born of fear always leaves a trail of restlessness. Urgency that pressures the spirit rarely comes from God.

Build routines that strengthen self-control even on days when emotions don't cooperate. Self-control is not a spontaneous talent, it is an invisible muscle built through consistent choices. Every act of discipline is like a brick placed in the foundation of your inner strength. When desire tries to take over, it is this hidden system that keeps you standing. Discipline is the invisible shield that protects your decision when your will wants to take control.

Learn to delay pleasures with a clear purpose. Emotional and spiritual maturity is revealed when you can distinguish what pleases you in the moment from what builds you in the long run. Not every pleasure is beneficial, and almost every pleasure that costs you peace is a well-disguised trap. Delaying gratification is not an act of denial, it is a conscious choice to prioritize what truly matters. It is planting without haste so you can reap without regret.

Walk with people who know how to wait. The rhythm of your soul is shaped by those who walk beside you. Surrounding yourself with anxious people is living in constant rush. But walking with the wise means experiencing a new rhythm: the rhythm of trust, maturity, and wisdom. The presence of those who live in God's timing calms the soul. The peace you breathe beside them soon starts manifesting in your own decisions.

Waiting is not a sign of weakness. It is the purest and most silent declaration of faith: I trust God's timing more than the urgency of my desires. Haste offers seductive shortcuts, but they are shortcuts with a high price. Only those who decide to wait, even when everything around them screams for action, will discover the right path, the perfect timing, and the purpose that is never lost along the way.

Chapter 4

The Wolf Disguised as Opportunity:

THE TEMPTATION THAT LOOKS LIKE A BLESSING

"Not every open door is opened by God. Some are traps disguised as opportunities."

The greatest danger of temptation is not in its face of error but in its mask of an answer. It does not present itself as a fall but as a chance. It does not offer what scares you, but what seduces you. It is a counterfeit blessing, with a forged divine seal and a hidden cost in fine print. The enemy does not work with impositions. He works with well-packaged suggestions. And some of the greatest downfalls began exactly like this: as something that looked like an answer to prayer.

The temptation that destroys you is not the one that frightens you. It is the one that convinces you. And it does not appear as something wrong. It appears as something urgent. As something that cannot wait. As a path that shines too brightly to be questioned. But the brighter the trail, the more caution you must have. Fake gold shines too. Disguised truth can feel soothing. And what brings comfort out of season can be poison with the flavor of peace.

How many decisions have been justified with apparent spirituality when, in reality, they were nothing more than emotional escapes? How many doors were embraced with faith but opened in haste? The human heart, says Jeremiah, is deceitful. And when desire grows strong, it begins to seek confirmation, not direction. Temptation, then, does not have to insist. It simply waves, and the heart, already seduced, does all the work of self-deception.

In the desert, while Moses received instructions from heaven, the people shaped an idol with their own hands. Not because they rejected God, but because they wanted a visible answer. Moses was taking too long. Anxiety screamed. And the golden calf was born from the combination of fear and haste. Idolatry, in that moment, was built with the intention of filling a divine silence with human noise.

Today, the justification has changed form but not essence. It takes phrases that sound spiritual: "I felt peace." "God opened this door." *"I believe He understands my moment."* But often, it is not peace, it is the absence of confrontation. It is not revelation, it is anxiety dressed as certainty. True faith never dispenses with discernment. Because not every sweet voice comes from God. And not every open door leads to life.

WHEN OPPORTUNITY IS A TRAP

Joseph was not simply facing a persistent woman. He was standing in the middle of a spiritual battlefield disguised with flattery and promises. In Genesis 39, we find a young foreigner who, despite having been sold as a slave, stood out for his integrity to the point of earning the total trust of Potiphar, his Egyptian master. It was a moment of rising success. And precisely there, where everything seemed to finally start going right, temptation came knocking.

Potiphar's wife did not seduce him with vulgar words but with a proposal wrapped in apparent protection. The invitation did not look like a pitfall but like a step toward favor. It did not appear as a fall but as a privilege. And that is why so many people stumble, because the most effective temptation does not present itself as wrong but as a justifiable exception. As maintenance of stability. As a reward for hard work.

Joseph, however, did not reason based on visible consequences. He stood firm because of an invisible principle, the fear of the Lord. He declared with clarity, *"How then could I do such a wicked thing and sin against God?"* (Genesis 39:9). His answer was not the result of rushed calculation but of a conviction matured long before the test arrived. He knew that those who negotiate values in the dark lose their authority in the light.

That door looked open, but it led to a cell. The invitation seemed like a prize, but it carried invisible chains. Not every opportunity that shines is divine. Some are polished chains with golden promises. What appeared to be stability was, in fact, disguised slavery. Joseph preferred to lose his palace position than to lose his standing before God.

This same pattern continues today, expressed with new language but the same poison. Leonardo, a young entrepreneur in the tech industry, received what seemed like an irresistible offer: a multimillion-dollar investment that would launch his startup to the international market. But there was a subtle clause in the contract, requiring him to compromise the ethical principles on which his company had been built. It looked like a technical requirement. But it was a subtle amputation of values.

Most people would have accepted with enthusiasm, calling it an open door, a blessing, a professional miracle. But Leonardo saw deeper. He understood that integrity is not an obstacle to growth, it is the foundation that prevents collapse. He turned down the offer. He lost the investment but kept his calling. A year later, his company was recognized worldwide for its unwavering ethics.

Joseph and Leonardo are not just examples of resistance. They are living proof that God honors those who place Him above any apparent advantage. The test is not only about what you gain but also about what you lose when you say "yes." Temptation, more often than not, is not after your immediate fall. It seeks your gradual surrender. And what begins as privilege often ends as prison.

WHY DO WE MAKE WRONG DECISIONS THINKING WE ARE RIGHT?

The most dangerous thing about wrong decisions is not their appearance but the conviction that accompanies them. It is when the heart says, "This is right," while the soul whispers, "This is not from God." The most effective temptation does not drag you away screaming, it convinces you with a smile. It takes advantage of invisible forces that shape our choices without us noticing.

1. The System of Anticipated Reward

Humans do not stumble because they are foolish but because they are driven by the sweet sensation of being close to achieving something extraordinary. It is not the prize itself that seduces, but the thrill of proximity. The brain, flooded with dopamine, starts confusing expectation with fulfillment. The problem? We often accept open doors that contradict our principles simply because the promised bonus feels irresistible. The salary increases, but the soul sinks.

2. False Autonomy in Decision-Making

We call freedom what is, in reality, escape. We label as "choice" what is nothing but desperation. How many times does someone start a new relationship not out of love but out of fear of loneliness? They call it a "new beginning" when, in truth, it is just an attempt to silence unresolved grief. We are not deciding with clarity, we are just trying to survive the emptiness within.

3. The Halo Effect

This psychological phenomenon distorts our perception. When something or someone has an initial shine (charisma, beauty, power), the brain creates a protective fog that hides the flaws. A legitimate advantage becomes the lens through which we interpret everything else. An investor falls in love with a partner's enthusiasm and overlooks abusive clauses. A Christian is dazzled by an apparent open door and ignores the warning signs. The initial charm erases the risks, like bright light hiding the cracks in the walls.

These three mechanisms work together as silent accomplices, shaping decisions that seem spiritual but are deeply emotional. It is not enough for a choice to feel right. It must be tested under the light of truth, conscience, and the peace that surpasses all understanding. The heart may be deceitful, but the Word is a lamp that exposes dangerous shortcuts. It is not a lack of intelligence that leads us to error. It is an excess of confidence in perceptions that we fail to discern.

HOW TO DISCERN BETWEEN BLESSING AND TRAP

Discernment requires more than sharp eyes, it requires a trained soul. Not everything that looks like a gift comes from heaven. Some offers shine on the outside but carry invisible thorns that wound the conscience.

1. Evaluate the Hidden Cost

True blessings never require you to sacrifice your essence. If, to receive something, you must give up your peace, compromise your values, or silence your conscience, you are not facing a gift, you are facing a test. Esau did not lose his inheritance because he was hungry. He lost it because he treated an eternal purpose as if it were just a common meal. When appetite governs your choice, destiny loses its value.

2. Observe the Fruits

Jesus was clear: every tree is known by its fruit. The Hebrew word peri, meaning fruit, points to the visible manifestation of an invisible root. If a decision preserves your integrity, nourishes your peace, and keeps your obedience intact, it bears the seal of divine approval. But if everything seems right except for the results that wound, destabilize, and dry up your faith, then the disguise is deeper than it appears. Appearance seduces, but time reveals.

3. Test the Peace That Comes with the Decision

God's peace is not the absence of external conflict. It is the presence of inner order. If what attracts you comes with unease, insomnia, and constant doubt, it is not the Spirit guiding you, it is anxiety pushing you. The enemy works with emotional urgency, while God moves with quiet convictions. Shalom does not mean mere calm but harmony between body, soul, and spirit. If peace cannot settle in your heart, it is a sign that the choice did not come from heaven.

4. Align with Eternal Principles

The book of Proverbs warns that there are ways that seem right to man, but their end is death. If moving forward requires you to bend Scripture, silence your conscience, or hide the truth, this is not the path God has set. Joseph resisted because he was not guided by favorable circumstances but by an unwavering faithfulness to the God who upheld him. He did not take shortcuts. He walked the narrow path of obedience.

Temptation does not simply want to offer you something. It wants to take you off your axis. That is why what looks like a promotion may be just a golden cell. Not all brightness points to heaven, sometimes it glows like a golden collar around the neck of someone who does not realize they are about to lose their freedom.

Discernment is a form of protection. Those who learn to discern protect the purpose they carry, the conscience that sustains them, and the future God has prepared.

THE GHOST OF THE EX:

THE TEMPTATION OF THE PAST THAT COMES BACK TO SABOTAGE YOUR PRESENT

"A traveler walks down a road he has traveled before. The path feels familiar, almost nostalgic. The stones that once made him stumble now seem smaller. The darkness that used to frighten him appears less threatening. He moves forward, convinced that this time it will be different. But at the end of the trail, he finds the very same trap that caught him in the past."

The past has a treacherous habit of presenting itself as a refuge. It does not arrive with chains or shouting but with subtle perfumes. It knows how to disguise itself perfectly, erasing the tears from your memories, silencing the cries of suffering, and framing everything with longing. What once destroyed your peace may now look like an unresolved chapter. That is exactly where danger lies: the past that returns in a new disguise still carries the same power to hold your soul captive.

There is a dangerous subtlety in this return. The past never comes back as it was but as our longing wishes it had been. In moments of fragility, the human mind becomes a sophisticated emotional editor. It does not present the facts with fidelity. It retells the story with convenient cuts, erases the tears, softens the screams, and highlights the hugs. It is like rewatching an old movie but with a soundtrack altered to make you feel again.

The danger is that by ignoring the full truth, the heart begins to negotiate with edited memories. What once hurt you now seems misunderstood. What destroyed your peace now sounds like a love that just never had the chance to happen. The captivity that once consumed you now returns disguised as freedom.

In this vulnerable state, three mental mechanisms begin to act stealthily:

- **Selective memory:** What used to be a cycle of pain is now remembered as intense passion. Betrayal is reframed as a misunderstanding. Manipulation is seen as concern. The brain delivers only what the heart is ready to romanticize.

- **The power of nostalgia:** Old emotions return with full force when triggered by subtle cues like a song, a social media post, or a photograph. But what returns is not reality. It is the comforting feeling our mind associated with those moments.

- **The deception of "it was better before":** On hard days, the past seems like a viable option. The filter of present pain paints yesterday with colors it never had. Israel, in the desert, forgot the chains and remembered only the meat. Egypt, which was a prison, started to be remembered as a feast.

THE BIBLE AND THE ECHOES OF THE PAST

AScripture does not just narrate the past. It interprets it, confronts it, and warns us about its disguised ghosts. There are times when returning to what was is not simply a relapse but a silent renunciation of what God is building. The stories that follow are not just old accounts. They act as prophetic mirrors, revealing the human heart and its tendency to negotiate with what should have already been left behind.

Egypt and the desire to go back reveal a paradox that remains current. Freedom requires responsibility, but slavery offers predictability. The people of Israel, faced with the discomfort of the journey, began to romanticize the pain they once begged to escape. *"If only we had died in Egypt, where we ate meat and bread..."* (Exodus 16:3). It was not true longing, but aversion to the process. Edited memory turned chains into comfort and slavery into safety. This mental mechanism is described clearly in Deuteronomy 8, where God warns about selective forgetting: *"Be careful that you do not forget the Lord after you eat and are satisfied..."* When the present is uncomfortable, the past gains flavors it never had.

Lot's wife was not turned into a pillar of salt because of a mere reflex. Her look back was a spiritual choice. She did not look out of curiosity but out of affection. The judgment was not just about a gesture but about a bond. Sodom represented everything God was destroying, and yet she still found it desirable. The Pentateuch, especially in Leviticus, presents the concept of "progressive holiness" as a process of continual separation from the profane. When she looked back, she was not just looking at a city but at a lifestyle. She refused to move forward with God. Those who refuse to move forward with the Lord end up frozen between past and judgment.

Peter, after denying Jesus, returned to the activity he knew: fishing. But it was not just a profession. It was his old identity. It was the refuge of his "before." After his failure, he went back to the sea, the very place where Jesus had called him to a higher purpose. And it was there that the risen Christ found him. The detail is significant: Jesus did not call him at the temple but at the place of his escape. This encounter echoes God's question to Elijah on Mount Horeb: *"What are you doing here, Elijah?"* (1 Kings 19:9). The temptation of the past is not just about repeating mistakes. It is about forgetting the calling. Peter was trying to catch fish again, but Jesus had called him to feed sheep. Going back is more than disobedience. It is underestimating the grace that lifts us up.

These three episodes — Egypt, Sodom, and the Sea of Galilee — show that the past does not need open gates. It only needs a willing heart. And many times, it comes back stronger when the present demands that we grow.

THE NEUROSCIENCE OF EMOTIONAL TRIGGERS

OThe past does not live only in memory. It inhabits the silent corridors of emotion, lying in wait for the right moment to be reactivated. It does not come with noise. It arrives quietly. Sometimes all it takes is a scent you did not even know you remembered, a song that plays by chance, or a casual conversation for doors that seemed sealed to open wide.

The big question is: why do we relive what we supposedly have already overcome? The answer lies in the invisible mechanisms of the brain, which archives emotions like old maps. These maps do not just remind us where we have been. They try to lead us back down familiar trails, even when those trails ended in cliffs. It is pain disguised as comfort. It is a prison with the scent of home.

Three silent neurological forces are at work in this process.

The hippocampus works as the black box of emotions. It does not record every moment equally. What lingers most are the experiences marked by intense pain or elevated pleasure. This is why a song, an old street, or a specific perfume can provoke strong physical and emotional reactions. Emotional memory does not ask logic for permission. It simply triggers what has been etched in the deepest part of the soul.

Imagine someone who has left an abusive relationship. Everything seemed resolved until a song playing by chance triggers not the pain but the memory of moments of affection. Even if those moments were rare, they were real. And that is enough for the memory to come tinted with longing rather than warning.

The hidden pleasure in pain is another treacherous mechanism. Dopamine, the neurotransmitter linked to reward, does not distinguish between healthy and destructive pleasure. It simply records the sensation. Toxic relationships, addictions, and compulsive behaviors leave marks because at some point they provided relief. Pain is forgotten, but the relief is remembered. Tears are ignored, but the embrace is replayed.

Toxic comfort may be the most dangerous of all. The human brain prefers known pain to the challenge of the unknown. Some people return to emotional prisons, destructive relationships, or old addictions not because they forgot the suffering but because the new does not yet feel safe. The predictability of chaos feels less frightening than the uncertainty of freedom.

People return to old patterns because the effort to change feels too high. The brain, in its quest to conserve energy, prefers to repeat routes even if they lead to collapse.

In the end, the past does not need an invitation. It only needs a crack. And the brain, deceived by its own circuits, can make something destructive feel strangely welcoming.

Discerning this trap requires more than willpower. It requires emotional awareness, spiritual clarity, and constant vigilance. Not every memory is a tribute. Some are traps disguised as longing.

"Discerning this trap requires more than willpower. It requires emotional awareness, spiritual clarity, and constant vigilance. Not every memory is a tribute. Some are traps disguised as longing."

HOW TO CLOSE THE DOOR OF THE PAST BEFORE IT SABOTAGES YOUR PRESENT

Discern between redemption and relapse. Not every reconnection means healing. In many cases, it is just a relapse disguised as something new. If what reappears in your life demands that you silence your conscience, lower your values, or forget your own story of overcoming, then it is not a new beginning. It is the same prison with freshly painted walls. And when a cell changes color but not purpose, it is still a cell.

Do not let the past whisper unchallenged. The past does not need to shout to be heard. It whispers during moments of vulnerability. That is why it is essential to strengthen spiritual awareness. A past that is not confronted will always repeat itself in the present. Pray before responding. Ask before opening the door. Reflect before accepting. The enemy does not need to be creative when he sees that the same shortcuts still work. If you tolerate a memory in your mind without confrontation, sooner or later it will govern your decisions again.

Detach from toxic nostalgia. Letting go of toxic nostalgia is an act of courage. If yesterday was defeated with tears, why welcome it back with smiles? What seems harmless today may steal your faith tomorrow. Those who walk toward purpose do not carry the shadows of the past. You cannot trade destiny for memory. You cannot exchange promise for nostalgia. The ticket back to captivity will always be cheaper than the cost of progress, but the long-term price is your soul.

Speak the language of the future. The way you speak reveals where you are looking. Adopt a language of future. Stop saying, "Back then I was happy," and start declaring with faith, "The best of God is still ahead of me." Your words are not just a reflection of your mind. They are the cradle of conviction. What you confess, your soul begins to build. And the place where your confession lives is the place where your steps will arrive.

Choose to advance. The past can teach, but it must never lead. It is a useful teacher but a cruel master. Every time longing knocks on your door, remember: not everything that calls you back comes to heal. Some voices from the past are just echoes of old prisons. What awaits you there is not a new chance, but the same cell with different decorations. Your decisions today draw the map of tomorrow. Those who choose to move forward do not return to revisit what once cost them their peace. Choose to move forward. Even if it hurts. Even if it costs. Even if going back feels easier. The future God has prepared is not behind you. It is on the path ahead.

THE TEMPTATION TO QUIT:

WHEN WEARINESS SPEAKS LOUDER THAN THE PROMISE

"A warrior can lose a battle without ever surrendering to the enemy. All it takes is for him to be tired enough to drop his sword. Discouragement does not come with a single blow. It drains strength little by little, emptying passion, silencing faith, and making every step heavier. Sometimes, the most dangerous temptation is not to sin. It is to give up."

The enemy does not always try to corrupt you with scandalous offers. Sometimes, all he needs is to keep you tired long enough for fatigue to replace faith. Weariness makes no noise. It accumulates like dust on forgotten furniture: imperceptible at first, suffocating in the end.

Many do not abandon great promises because of error, but because of exhaustion. The adversary's main strategy is not always to lead you into sin, but to drain you until giving up seems like the only sensible option.

How many times has your soul wanted to sit down in the middle of the path?

- A leader who once began with passion but now feels the crushing weight of responsibility.

- A marriage that was once full of hope but has become a silent war.

- A ministry, a dream, or a journey that once felt divine but now seems to punish more than strengthen.

Silent exhaustion clouds vision, distorts reality, turns mountains into walls, and silences the song of promise into murmurs of discouragement.

WHEN EXHAUSTION BECOMES A TRAP

Burnout does not invade like a thief breaking down doors. It approaches like a poisonous whisper, dripping slowly over emotions until the spirit, once vibrant, begins to hibernate under the weight of its own fatigue. What was once just a step now looks like a cliff. What was once a pause now becomes paralysis. And by the time you realize it, you are already surrounded by walls built with the bricks of your own surrender.

The mind, under the subtle grip of fatigue, stops discerning the present accurately. The soul's lenses become foggy. Small things, once solvable with faith and focus, now take on apocalyptic proportions. Situations that once required only patience now feel like a battle for survival. What once seemed unthinkable — quitting — starts presenting itself as a rational, even sensible, option.

What extreme exhaustion causes in you:

It distorts reality. Weariness does not just drain energy. It intoxicates perspective. What was simply a delay yesterday now sounds like imminent failure. A "no" feels like a certificate of incompetence. Small mistakes seem like a final condemnation. Exhaustion paints the world with shades of despair, and even the holiest promises feel too distant to be real.

It reduces resilience. The soul, wounded by an accumulation of unprocessed battles, gradually loses its ability to start over. A stumble that once inspired learning now reinforces old fears. Patience dissolves like mist under the sun. Hope becomes as fragile as a thread about to snap. Obstacles that should be steppingstones now turn into colossal walls. Emotionally, life becomes a minefield where any step feels like it could be the last.

It muffles the voice of God. Fatigue has its own noise. It is not loud, but constant. It is like a spiritual hum that fills every corner of the soul, making it hard to hear what is eternal. You pray but feel like you are shouting into an empty valley. You read Scripture, but the words seem like mere ink on paper. God's presence is still there, unchanged, but your spiritual sensitivity has been numbed. The veil is not over heaven but over your eyes. Exhaustion creates a deafening silence, not because God stopped speaking, but because you stopped listening.

And the most dangerous part: you do not have to fall into temptation to lose your purpose. You just have to become so empty that the vision disappears. You just have to let go of the sword, not because the enemy defeated you, but because you no longer see a reason to hold it.

THE BIBLE AND WEARY WARRIORS

OExhaustion does not choose its victims based on visible scars or spiritual medals. It does not respect a record of miracles or a reputation for faith. Often, it strikes those who seemed unshakable. Men who were pillars in times of crisis, voices in deserts of unbelief, bridges over great chasms. Yet, at some point in their journey, their inner strength began to dry up like streams under the scorching sun.

Elijah: From Victory to Depression. Elijah was no ordinary prophet. He was a man who walked between fire and heaven, who faced kings and mocked idols, who prayed and saw the sky answer with fire on the altar. On Mount Carmel, when fire fell and consumed the sacrifice before an entire nation, Elijah seemed untouchable. Yet, shortly after, this same man fled. He hid. He sat under a tree and cried out, *"Enough, Lord. Take my life"* (1 Kings 19:4).

The great victory of the previous day was drowned out by the weariness of his soul and fear in his heart. Elijah forgot what God had done yesterday and began to fear what might happen tomorrow. It happens to us too. Public glory does not immunize us from private collapses. What you conquered yesterday does not eliminate your need for renewal today.

Maybe you feel like that too. You won battles with your hands, but you are losing with your heart. Yet God did not judge Elijah for his exhaustion. He fed him with warm bread. He let him sleep. He spoke in a gentle whisper. Before giving him a new mission, God provided rest. Sometimes, your greatest need is not to run harder, but to let God heal you in the desert.

Moses: The Leader Who Asked for Relief. Moses witnessed the impossible. He saw the sea split, the plagues strike an empire, manna fall from heaven. He heard God's voice on the mountain, in the fire, in the cloud. But one day, the burden of leadership became too heavy. The constant murmuring of an ungrateful people began to wear down the soul of the liberator. Until he cried out in despair, *"If this is how you are going to treat me, please go ahead and kill me now"*(Numbers 11:15).

It was not disbelief. It was overload. It was not rebellion. It was exhaustion. Moses did not want to abandon his faith, he just wanted rest from the weight of leading people who seemed more attached to Egypt than to the promise.

How many today feel the same cry within? People carrying entire families, businesses, ministries. People who were once pillars of strength but are now sinking into silence because the weight has become unbearable. Moses teaches us that even giants of faith can bend. The secret is not to try to be a hero without wounds. It is to acknowledge that even the most glorious calling needs shared shoulders. God did not abandon him. God raised seventy to help him. No mission was meant to be carried alone.

Jeremiah: The Prophet Who Almost Went Silent. Jeremiah carried God's word like fire in his bones. He was chosen before birth, anointed to be a voice in a corrupt generation. But being faithful to the truth cost him everything: friends, acceptance, security. Persecuted, mocked, alone, he reached the point of saying, *"I will not mention His word or speak anymore in His name"* (Jeremiah 20:9).

Fatigue tried to silence prophecy. Pain tried to bury his calling. But the Word was stronger than the fatigue. It burned inside him like fire shut up in his bones. He tried to quit, but he could not. Because a true calling cannot retire due to exhaustion. It rises from the ashes when everything else goes quiet.

Jeremiah shows us that it is not the absence of pain that validates a calling. It is the impossibility of walking away from it. When what God placed inside you burns hotter than any rejection around you, the mission continues, even with tears in your eyes and weariness in your soul.

THE SCIENCE OF EMOTIONAL FATIGUE

Burnout is not just physical pain that a few hours of sleep can fix. It is a collapse of meaning. An internal rupture between what you do and why you do it. Yes, the body feels it. But it is the mind that fails. It is the soul that cries.

Neuroscientific studies reveal that continuous fatigue deeply alters brain function. The prefrontal cortex, responsible for ethical decisions, self-control, creativity, and planning, suffers a kind of emotional blackout. What was once clear becomes blurry. Faith weakens, not because of lack of content, but because of excessive weight. It is like trying to see the sky through a fogged-up window.

Creativity, which once was a refuge, now feels like an empty room.

Resilience, which once held you up in crises, crumbles at the slightest impact.

Optimism, which once fueled your soul, dissolves into automatic thoughts of defeat.

And the most alarming part: a tired mind is vulnerable to distorted narratives. It accepts as truth what faith would reject if there were energy. It starts believing that stopping is wisdom, when in reality it is just weariness speaking louder. It trades discernment for quitting. According to researchers at Stanford University, this is not just linked to the intensity of activities but to the absence of visible purpose.

The human mind was not designed just to carry loads. It was created to sustain meaning. When the "why" disappears, any "what" becomes unbearable. Burnout, so common today, is the soul protesting against becoming a worker of a mission that has lost its inner light.

That is why true rest is not just a break. It is a reconnection. A soul without purpose turns work into torture and each day into torment. But when purpose is reignited, even the burden feels lighter. The reminder of your calling renews strength. The awareness that God is still writing your story reignites hope.

You were not called just to endure. You were called to remember.

What moved you in the beginning is still enough to sustain you at the end.

Rediscover the meaning and you will rediscover strength.

HOW TO RENEW YOUR STRENGTH BEFORE FATIGUE WINS

Recognize the early signs of exhaustion. Collapse does not start with your body on the ground but with your soul going silent. Exhaustion often disguises itself as routine, productivity, or unrelenting faithfulness. It hides behind mechanical smiles and commitments completed on autopilot. But inside, the heart is already sending signals of emotional breakdown. When fatigue becomes part of your identity, denial becomes its ally. What is denied by the mind is cultivated in the subconscious like a ticking time bomb. Breakdown is the final cry of a soul that has been silently pleading for help.

Share the burden. Your calling may be heavenly, but your limits are human. Even Jesus, the Son of God, accepted help under the weight of the cross. That was not weakness. It was wisdom. Moses, the liberator of an entire people, almost broke not because of Pharaoh's opposition but because of the weight of lonely leadership. It was God who commanded relief, not weakness. The idea of carrying everything alone is not nobility, it is a trap. Pride pretends to be strength but isolates, exhausts, and eventually destroys. Sharing the weight is not a sign of spiritual failure, it is a divine strategy for emotional survival. Any mission carried by a single heart will eventually carry a collapsing body.

Seek renewal in God's presence, not just in rest. Sleep relieves muscle tension, but it does not restore the soul's depth. Elijah rested under a tree, but he was only lifted up when he heard God whispering in the silence of the cave. God's presence is not an optional devotional add-on. It is oxygen for those carrying destinies. A pillow may calm the body, but only the altar restores the essence. Many are rested in body but dead inside because they confused rest with restoration. It is not the absence of movement that heals. It is the presence of the Eternal that revives.

Change how you interpret the journey. The difference between trauma and testimony lies in how you interpret pain. Gold does not curse fire. It understands that fire is necessary. The vine does not reject pruning. It knows that fruit comes from it. Some pains are not signs of abandonment but evidence of preparation. Those who see every adversity as rejection will live wounded. But those who see it as training will come out stronger. Not every tear needs to be wiped away immediately. Some need to be understood. They do not signal failure. They reveal the forge.

Reconnect with your original purpose. Every mission carried with a broken heart is a reminder that what drives you is not comfort, it is calling. Peter was not restored by a miracle but by a question that cut deep: "Do you love Me?" God does not restore soldiers with techniques. He restores children with questions that pierce the core of their motivation. The fire that was born in heaven does not die on earth. What made you start is still alive, even when everything around you feels dead. When passion is rekindled, the weight remains, but your strength is renewed.

Discouragement is the echo of hope that lost its address. But God knows the way back.

The promise is not measured by the weight of the burden, but by the faithfulness of the One who made it.

When exhaustion pushes you to quit, choose to rest, but never surrender what heaven entrusted to you.

Rest with awareness. Rise with conviction. Those who learn to rest without surrender will one day rise to conquer what once seemed unreachable.

Chapter 7

THE GAME OF MANIPULATION:

WHEN TEMPTATION IS NOT A SIN, BUT A PERSON

"Some temptations do not live inside you. They walk beside you, look into your eyes, and say exactly what you want to hear. Not every down-fall starts with a desire. Some begin with a connection."

The most sophisticated temptation is not the one that openly invites you to sin, but the one that presents itself as someone who claims to have your best interests at heart. The devil does not always appear through obvious pleasures or blatant proposals. Sometimes, he simply places a person in your path. Someone who praises you just enough, who seems to understand you better than anyone else, who supports you exactly when everyone else confronts you. A person who becomes indispensable in your daily life, so present and so available that, little by little, they start to redraw your boundaries. And without realizing it, you begin erasing the line between what is right and what is simply convenient.

That is why this kind of temptation is so dangerous: it does not look like sin. It disguises itself as friendship, as "honest advice," as emotional support. It is not a sudden fall but a gradual surrender. You do not stumble; you give in. Out of affection. Out of fear. Out of gratitude.

Have you ever considered that the temptation threatening your spiritual life most might have a proper name?

- It is not just explicit pornography. It is the friend who normalizes impurity, trivializes holiness, and calls the pursuit of purity religious fanaticism.

- It is not just an occasional doubt. It is that persistent voice that chips away at your faith, whispering uncertainties disguised as rationality, until trusting God feels naïve.

- It is not just the desire for forbidden pleasure. It is the seemingly wise advice that pulls you away from your purpose, using practicality as an excuse to escape obedience.

- It is not just malice that destroys. It is "excessive care" that suffocates your convictions, as if self-protection were more important than obedience.

- Temptation does not need to scream, "abandon your faith." It just whispers, "compromise a little... for the sake of love, peace, or unity." And little by little, your principles are negotiated until they disappear.

The enemy does not always want to convince you. Sometimes, he only wants to surround you. Because when control is no longer in your hands but in someone else's influence, sin does not need to be planted. It only needs to be cultivated with your permission.

Have you ever felt like you were doing something wrong but could not pinpoint where you lost your balance? Have you ever sensed that someone was leading you to a place you would never have chosen on your own, but somehow it felt inevitable?

Welcome to the game of manipulation. And in this game, if you do not realize you are being moved, you are already losing.

HEARTS LED BY HANDS THAT SHOULD NEVER GUIDE

Some moves do not happen on the field of reason but on the stage of emotions. One of the most dangerous temptations does not enter through the door of logic but through the window of the heart. It does not come shouting. It comes smiling. And little by little, the one who was called to be the protagonist of a destiny becomes a mere supporting character in a narrative the enemy wrote.

It is in this subtle setting that manipulation reveals its darkest face. It is not about a sudden fall but a progressive steering. When the heart is given into the wrong hands, it begins to be shaped by affections that seem genuine but hide distorted intentions. Decisions are no longer born from deep convictions but from emotional responses to ties forged with someone who should never have had such influence over your soul.

This is where we find two of the most striking portraits in Scripture: Samson and Ahab. Men who were anointed, called, powerful in the eyes of others, but who were defeated from the inside out. They were not taken down by armed enemies but by relationships that drained their spiritual authority. They did not fall because they were weak but because they handed control to those who were never meant to direct their choices.

Samson's fall began with a voice that wore him down before destroying him. Samson was not defeated by a sword or caught in an ambush. His fall was not sudden but carefully built through gestures that looked like affection, words that sounded like care, and emotional bonds that should never have grown that deep.

Delilah did not confront his strength. She never wielded weapons or shouted commands. She simply surrounded him with affection. Slowly, she dismantled what upheld his resistance. She diluted his focus, weakened his spiritual vigilance, and dimmed the flame of his purpose. What she took from him was not just a secret. She stole the root of his identity, the source of his anointing, the living reminder of his calling.

The strategy was not violent. It was calculated. She did not impose. She seduced. She did not intimidate with threats but captivated with affection. Her persistence was disguised as concern, her tenderness masked sharp intentions. When love is removed from its true center, it becomes the most fatal of traps.

Samson's fall did not begin with the scissors. It started with silent compromises, tolerated conversations, impulsive answers, and boundaries that were gradually loosened like knots that unravel without warning. His strength was not taken all at once. It was surrendered in small doses, in choices, in careless slips. Until nothing was left but a strong body with no soul to sustain it.

The man who once struck down a thousand with a donkey's jawbone was defeated by himself. Not by outward brutality but by inner neglect. What destroyed him was not the violence outside but the seduction he chose to keep close.

The tragedy of his story lies not only in his fall but in the subtle way it began. He underestimated the small things, and because of that, he lost the great. The thread of his strength was broken within long before it was cut on the surface.

Today's Delilahs do not use scissors. They use words that relativize. They do not appear as forbidden lovers but as colleagues who play with integrity. They show up as counselors who disguise shortcuts with practical wisdom, as mentors who trade truth for convenience.

They do not break alliances with visible violence but with whispered justifications. They do not demand open betrayal but gently suggest small compromises. They do not say "abandon your faith" but murmur "be less rigid." They ask for just one step away from what you believe and one step closer to what you will tolerate.

Every tolerated compromise is a crack in the wall. Every silence in the face of wrong is a brick removed from your fortress. Every emotional argument that replaces a spiritual conviction is another invisible thread that snaps.

Manipulation does not knock on the door like a declared enemy. It enters like a welcomed guest. It chips away at your vigilance until you drop the sword yourself. Whoever ignores the warning signs today will mourn the loss of strength tomorrow. Spiritual collapse does not begin with scandals. It begins with conversations that should never happen. With principles left unspoken. With tiny deviations that pave the way for ruin.

What is tolerated in secret will be what exposes you in public. What temptation whispers today will be shouted as shame tomorrow.

And this game does not end with Samson. It only changes strategy. Because when manipulation does not work on the heart, it tries to dominate the mind. If Delilah emptied Samson from within, Jezebel rewrote Ahab's decisions from without.

Jezebel turned power into corruption by using Ahab. Ahab wore the crown but did not rule. His title was real, but his heart was surrendered. Authority still rested on his head, but the command had already been transferred to other hands. Jezebel did not need a war to seize the throne. She conquered it through influence.

When Naboth refused to sell his vineyard, Ahab reacted like a child who did not get the toy he wanted. He sulked, turned his face to the wall, and refused to eat. Jezebel, however, saw in the king's weakness an opportunity to take control. She devised the plan, wrote the letters, manipulated the leaders. Ahab? He simply agreed. He just watched. He just let it happen.

Ahab's fall did not begin with Naboth's blood spilled in the field. It began much earlier, when he gave up discernment and handed over the reins of his conscience to someone who should never have ruled it. It was not the criminal act that destroyed him. It was his passivity toward evil. It was the cowardice before manipulation. It was the silence of a man who should have protected principles but preferred to preserve convenience.

Jezebel knew exactly what Ahab wanted. And she gave it to him. But the price was charged in invisible installments, spread over time, corroding his integrity before he realized it. This is the most subtle essence of manipulation. It does not demand a throne immediately. It is content to sit beside it, until the true king forgets who is supposed to lead.

Today's Jezebels do not plot in palaces. They whisper in needy relationships, in compliments that feed the ego, in conversations that sound like support but hide control. They do not break down doors. They enter through emotional wounds, through the need for validation, through the longing to be understood. And they build alliances disguised as protection, but which are chains with delicate ties.

Jezebels do not give orders directly. They shape choices with sweet words. They do not dominate by force. They dominate by permission. And slowly, the one who should rule over their own decisions ends up obeying commands that never came from God.

If Samson was defeated by giving his heart to someone who did not deserve his trust, Ahab was defeated by delegating his conscience to someone who knew no limits. In both cases, the outcome was the same. The ruin came not from the outside but from within. The throne, which should have been a symbol of authority, became a stage for slavery disguised as partnership.

Manipulation does not invade. It takes over the space where vigilance is absent. And whoever does not guard the door of their heart will sooner or later find the enemy writing the chapters of their own story.

HOW TO BECOME STRONGER AGAINST MANIPULATION

Recognize the signs before they turn into invisible chains. A manipulator rarely starts with demands. They begin with disguised tests. These are gestures of apparent care that quietly overstep your boundaries. These are suggestions that imperceptibly violate your principles. These are feelings of discomfort that arise without explanation, but your soul already recognizes them as warnings. What seems like a simple opinion today may become a command tomorrow. What looks like mere closeness might be the start of emotional control. Intuition is the whisper God sends before the disaster shouts. Ignoring it is like closing your eyes on a road that ends in a cliff.

Learn to say "no" without guilt or unnecessary explanations. Manipulation thrives where there is insecurity about taking a stand. If someone needs to persuade you to accept what your conscience rejects, then your answer should already be "no." Saying "no" is not an offense. It is an act of loyalty to your identity. Integrity is not only shown in the actions we take but in the wrong turns we refuse. Every "no" you give to error preserves a "yes" that will be needed when God's purpose calls for clarity and strength. Saying no is resisting the silent theft of your essence.

Establish boundaries that protect your identity. True love respects boundaries. Genuine respect does not push past clearly defined limits. But a manipulator interprets boundaries as challenges to overcome. They test your tolerance. They stretch what you called non-negotiable. They try to paint your walls with guilt. If someone does not respect your "no," the problem is not your firmness but the quiet intrusion you are allowing. A healthy boundary does not isolate. It preserves. It does not build walls against communion but against invasions disguised as companionship.

Do not fear disappointing those who were only there to use you. Manipulation does not grieve your absence. It only misses the control it once had. The manipulator does not regret your pain. They regret your resistance. Therefore, do not feel guilty for frustrating the expectations of someone who was always willing to hurt you for convenience. The true loss is not breaking ties with those who drain your essence. It is losing yourself in the attempt to be loved by someone who never saw you with the right eyes. Preserving your truth is more valuable than keeping the company of those who trade affection for control.

Remember: temptation does not always shout.
Sometimes it smiles. It does not come knocking on doors
or making demands. It comes offering comfort, listening
to your pain, saying exactly what you wanted to hear. And
little by little, their advice turns into orders, their opinions into commands, and your story starts being rewrit-
ten with words that were never inspired by God. Those
who never learn to say "no" to the wrong people will end
up saying "yes" to the wrong chapters of their own journey. It is not the shouts that mislead the most. It is the
smiles that confuse the most.

**Guard your heart as if protecting the center of a
besieged city.** The most dangerous attack does not always
come head-on. Sometimes, it approaches in the form of an
embrace. Manipulation does not destroy with violence. It
dissolves convictions with distorted affection. The problem is not in what the person asks but in what they subtly
suggest. And when you give too much ground out of fear
of losing, you have already lost what matters most: your
inner freedom. Guard your heart not only from your own
desires but from the voices that, while smiling, lead you
away from the path you were created to walk.

Chapter 8

THE POWER OF ENVY:

THE TEMPTATION OF WANTING WHAT
BELONGS TO SOMEONE ELSE

"Envy never presents itself as an innocent desire. It begins as a silent unease, a discomfort disguised as fairness, a seed growing in the shadows. At first, it feels like nothing more than a passing frustration. But before you realize it, you are measuring your life by someone else's ruler, turning another person's achievements into thorns in your own flesh. Envy does not just desire what others have. It feeds on the emptiness of the one who carries it."

Envy is an invisible fire. It does not begin with a shout but with a suffocated sigh. It does not arise in storms but in disguised breezes. As you walk the road of your dreams, it places stones in your shoes. As you celebrate small victories, it whispers that they are insignificant. At first, it seems like just a brief discomfort, a distracted glance at your neighbor's yard. But envy never wants to simply observe. It wants to possess. And when it cannot have, it tries to destroy.

This is the silent drama of envy: it does not just want what the other person has. It wants the other to lose what they have. It is not enough to achieve; it must also discredit those who got there first. It is not enough to grow; it must hope the other shrinks. Envy disguises itself as a thirst for justice, but deep down, it is nothing but a thirst for center stage. It dresses up as healthy ambition, but it is dormant rot. It starts as a legitimate feeling of "I want that too," but quickly transforms into "if I can't have it, may no one else have it either."

The poison of envy does not kill at once. It seeps through comparisons, silent frustrations, and the addiction of measuring your worth by the success of others. Every victory from someone else feels like your personal defeat. Every applause that isn't yours sounds like rejection. Every blessing that isn't yours feels like injustice. And all the while, silently, your soul begins to corrode until what was once admiration becomes a prison.

The greatest tragedy of envy is not that it keeps you from having more. It is that it prevents you from being whole. Because anyone who builds their happiness on another's unhappiness is actually digging their own grave without realizing it. Envy does not just rob you of what you could achieve. It robs you of what you should already be celebrating.

THE ANATOMY OF ENVY

AThe temptation of envy does not explode like thunder. It creeps in like a whisper. It does not knock you down like an avalanche. It corrodes like silent rust, imperceptible, until the soul's structure is weakened.

While some people are building with their own hands, the envious person builds prisons with their thoughts. While others celebrate genuine victories, the envious one collects resentments like invisible trophies, trading the freedom of their own journey for an obsession with monitoring someone else's.

Eternal wisdom warns us:

"A heart at peace gives life to the body, but envy rots the bones." (Proverbs 14:30)

This rotting does not happen overnight. It is a subtle, almost imperceptible process, and that is precisely what makes it so deadly. Envy builds its silent empire in stages, starting with an invisible seed, then fermenting in secret until it poisons an entire identity. To understand the danger it poses, we must dissect its stages and see how a small concession can grow into silent destruction.

The Silent Birth is when comparison disguises itself as admiration. It all starts innocently. You celebrate someone's achievement, but soon after, a sneaky question whispers in your soul: "What about me? When will it be my turn?" Comparison is born when admiration loses its purity. The happiness for someone else's success is invaded by a shadow of restlessness.

Example: A friend gets promoted, and instead of simply celebrating, you feel a heavy discomfort in your chest. It is not hate. It is not bad will. It is just that nagging whisper: "I deserved it too." The problem is not the other's celebration. It is the distorted lens that starts warping how you see your own journey.

The Fermentation of Resentment happens when the heart starts counting invisible debts. What began as discomfort evolves into persistent resentment. The success of others stops being an inspiring testimony and becomes a cruel reminder of what you have not achieved yet. Every victory now feels like a personal attack on your dignity.

Example: You see someone posting about their success, and it feels like each post is a personal provocation, a public humiliation of your "delay." Resentment is the silent fertilizer that feeds envy. It is not that the other person is celebrating to humiliate you. It is that your heart is already too wounded to celebrate with them.

The Rationalization of Dissatisfaction is revealed in the slow construction of poisonous excuses.

This stage is when you start minimizing someone else's achievements to protect your ego.

"He only got there because he was lucky."

"She only achieved that because of her connections."

This rationalization works like emotional anesthesia, numbing the inner pain without healing it. The envious person finds comfort in devaluing others because they no longer find motivation within themselves.

Example: Someone watches a colleague pull off a huge project, but instead of learning from it, mutters under their breath: "It's easy for him. I'd like to see him in my shoes." Rationalization does not fix real injustice. It only feeds the bitterness of imagined injustice.

The Erosion of Identity begins when life turns into a constant competition. The final stage is the most tragic. Envy stops being just a feeling. It becomes a way of living. The envious person no longer dreams their own dreams. They live to try to outdo others. Their identity is not built on their purpose but on the obsession of not falling behind.

Example: A person abandons their calling just to prove they can be as successful as the one they admire or envy. But deep down, the victory they seek will never fill the emptiness of someone who lost themselves in the process.

When identity is shaped by silent competition, every win is a fleeting relief, and every loss a devastating sentence. Envy is the silent architect of inner ruins. Every comparison not confronted grows. Every resentment not addressed takes root. Every rationalization left unchallenged builds an invisible prison. And in the end, the envious person discovers that their greatest loss was not the opportunity of another, but their own freedom to be who they were meant to be.

CHAPTERS LOST TO ENVY

The Bible does not shy away from the poison of envy. On the contrary, it shows how envy was the invisible thread that stitched together some of humanity's greatest tragedies. Envy did not just kill dreams. It killed destinies. It did not only hurt those envied. It destroyed those who gave in to it.

Cain and Abel: When Comparison Turns into Deadly Hatred. Cain did not just want his offering to be accepted by God. He wanted to be exalted above his brother. When he saw Abel receive favor from the Lord, envy began to ferment inside him like a simmering rage. The rejection of his own offering was not seen as an invitation to change but as a public humiliation. God warned Cain: "Sin is crouching at your door; it desires to have you, but you must rule over it." But Cain chose to kill his brother rather than change himself. How many times do people today attack those who move forward rather than fixing what keeps them from growing? When someone else's success threatens you more than it inspires you, you are no longer fighting for your purpose. You are fighting against yourself.

Saul and David: When a Song Awakens the Worst in the King's Heart. Saul was God's anointed. A king crowned by divine will. But the moment he heard the women of Israel singing about David — "Saul has slain thousands, and David tens of thousands" — his heart became contaminated. Envy turned Saul into a prisoner of his own bitterness. Instead of ruling, he started chasing. Instead of protecting his throne, he tried to destroy the future. The song did not take Saul's reign away. But envy destroyed him from the inside out. How often do leaders, pastors, or entrepreneurs see talent rise and, instead of mentoring it, try to crush it out of fear of being overshadowed? Envy never protects what you have. It only corrodes even what you have already achieved.

Joseph's Brothers: When Hatred for Someone's Success Becomes a Project of Destruction. Joseph did not ask to be the favorite son. He did not choose to have grand dreams. But his brothers, unable to handle the favor he carried, decided it would be better to eliminate him. Envy did not just blind them. It dehumanized them. They plotted his death, then sold him as a slave. The colorful coat was just a piece of fabric, but to them, it symbolized everything they deemed unfair and intolerable. Yet the plan of the envious never cancels God's purpose. Joseph was thrown into a pit, sold into slavery, and forgotten in prison. But God raised him to become governor of Egypt. The irony of envy is this: while the envious are plotting someone else's ruin, God is turning pain into a platform.

Envy does not just harm the envied. In the end, it destroys those who chose it as a silent companion. It builds emotional prisons with walls of comparison and resentment. Those who fail to overcome envy do not just lose others. They lose themselves — and often the future God wanted to place in their hands.

THE INVISIBLE EFFECT OF SOCIAL MEDIA AND THE SUBTLE POISON OF MODERN COMPARISON

Once limited to the corridors of daily life, envy has now gained digital wings, spreading in seconds across screens. Social media does not reveal reality. It projects curated storefronts, shaped by filters, angles, and rehearsed captions. It is a staged performance where everything shines, but almost nothing is true. And the brain, with no time to discern reality from fabrication, interprets these images as undeniable evidence that everyone is living better than you.

It is not just about observing someone else's happiness but being bombarded with a constant flow of achievements, trips, smiles, and celebrations. Hardly anyone posts failures, existential crises, or days of pain.

And since the human mind tends to absorb what it sees without filtering the context, we end up comparing our behind-the-scenes with someone else's highlight reel. Ordinary life becomes shameful. Gratitude fades. And what was once enough suddenly feels insignificant.

Behavioral psychology studies show that this dynamic is quietly destructive. More than 60% of users report a drop in self-esteem, and about 39% admit feeling envy when seeing content from people who appear to be constantly successful. The problem worsens with what is called "upward comparison," when we measure ourselves against unreachable standards. It not only feeds frustration but also triggers depression, especially among women and teenagers. What was once a mere pinch of discomfort now becomes internal corrosion of identity.

Studies reveal that teenagers who spend more than three hours a day on these platforms are twice as likely to develop severe symptoms of anxiety and depression. The brain, exposed to unrealistic standards of beauty, success, and happiness, begins to normalize the unattainable. And what should be just a distraction becomes an emotional prison. Every missed like feels like rejection. Every perfect post from someone else confirms your own failure.

This cycle is not just psychological. It is spiritual. A soul fed on comparisons loses its ability to rejoice in what it has. The most dangerous part is that this poison comes disguised as entertainment. The glow of the screen, once a companion, becomes a silent enemy. The feeling that everyone else is moving forward while you remain still traps the mind in an emotional cell with no windows.

The culture of external validation only deepens this scenario. When your identity depends on the gaze of others, every digital reaction becomes a verdict of worth. There is always someone with more followers, more applause, more trips, more beauty. And when your worth is measured by that stage, you condemn yourself to a life marked by scarcity of purpose and constant feelings of inadequacy.

The seriousness of this extends beyond emotions. According to data from the World Health Organization, more than 11% of teenagers show problematic behaviors linked to social media, including social isolation, low self-esteem, and suicidal thoughts. The story of Molly Russell, a 14-year-old British girl who took her own life after consuming harmful content online, is a warning to us all. Between 2008 and 2021, cases of hospitalization for self-harm among girls increased by 70%, revealing a silent crisis beneath the surface of pretty posts and empty motivational quotes.

Digital envy does not destroy all at once. It corrodes slowly. It breaks the bridge of gratitude, empties the value of personal achievements, and distorts the reflection of one's own identity. Gradually, without realizing it, the heart begins to crave what others have and despise what God has already placed in your hands. We consume other people's dreams as daily bread while forgetting to recognize God's work in our own story.

HOW TO BREAK THE CYCLE OF ENVY AND BUILD A SECURE IDENTITY

Envy does not disappear when you acquire more. It disappears when you stop measuring your life by someone else's ruler. The problem was never what others have. The real problem has always been how you interpret it within yourself. As long as your identity depends on comparison, there will be a void that no achievement can fill. Even if you have everything, you will still feel as though you have nothing.

Learn to celebrate other people's victories. Someone else's success does not diminish yours. If you cannot rejoice in others' achievements, you are not yet ready to live your own victories. Envy prevents you from celebrating. And those who do not know how to celebrate will never be celebrated. Someone else's success may be a sign that God is working in that area, not a threat to what He will still do in your life. Those who applaud today, without envy, open the way to be applauded tomorrow without burden.

Develop an abundance mindset. The envious see the world as an arena where only a few can prosper. But this vision is a trap. In God's Kingdom, there is enough room for everyone to grow. Another's blessing does not diminish yours. But envy can diminish you. As long as you interpret someone else's victory as a threat, you will never recognize the value of the blessings already quietly blooming within your own story.

Redefine what success means for you. If your idea of success is based on being better than others, frustration will be endless. There will always be someone ahead. Someone who arrived faster, shined brighter, or received more recognition. True success is not about impressing a fickle audience but about fulfilling the purpose Heaven wrote for you. Those who live to impress others will always be slaves to public opinion. Those who live to fulfill a calling will be free even when ignored.

Envy might make you look at others and feel smaller. But an identity rooted in God will make you look inside and realize you already carry everything you need to grow. Someone else's light does not dim yours. Someone else's success does not diminish the promise resting on your life. The real victory is not in being faster, more famous, or more applauded. It is in being more faithful to what God has placed inside you.

Chapter 9

THE CODE OF RESISTANCE:

HOW TO OVERCOME TEMPTATION BEFORE IT DEFEATS YOU

"No castle falls with a single blow. No warrior gives up after the first battle. Defeat begins much earlier, in the small cracks ignored, in the walls left unreinforced, in the naïve confidence that the structure will withstand any attack. Temptation does not destroy suddenly. It tests, weakens, and wears down until the right moment arrives. Whoever expects to win on the battlefield without having trained beforehand has already lost without realizing it."

Resisting is not an instinctive reflex. It is a deliberate construction. The battle does not begin at the moment of the indecent proposal, the subtle invitation, or the enticing offer. It begins long before, in the way you structure your mind, your routine, and your soul. The true code of resistance is built when no one is watching. It is the sum of silent decisions that later become unbreakable shields.

Temptation rarely takes on a grotesque form. It wears the disguise of immediate relief, comforting company, and convincing excuses. It comes smiling. It promises consolation. And, subtly, it begins to corrode the inner structure. When the mind is tired, when the spirit has been neglected, and when emotions are fragile, even the most solid principles become negotiable.

Samson, anointed and feared, fell not because temptation was stronger than him, but because his preparation was far too weak. Raw strength does not save those who despise vigilance. Joseph, on the other hand, overcame not because he was untouchable, but because he anticipated danger. He fled before the mind became entangled. And by fleeing, he did not lose strength; he gained authority. What separates those who fall from those who resist is not the absence of temptation but the presence of preparation.

The question was never if temptation will come. It will come. And it does not choose a convenient time. It can appear at the height of exhaustion, at the peak of success, or in the silence of unconfessed loneliness. The real question is: will you be ready when it knocks? Neuroscience reveals something surprising: decisions are made in the unconscious up to seven seconds before they become conscious. This means that when you say "no," your brain has already followed a route of habits formed long before. The visible choice is merely the reflection of thousands of invisible micro-decisions accumulated over time.

Temptation does not win at the moment of confrontation. It triumphs or is defeated in the days before, in neglected routines, in thoughts nurtured in secret, in the boundaries we fail to draw for fear of seeming radical or inflexible. What seems like a sudden stumble is often just the final stage of a silent collapse that has been building for days, months, or even years.

This chapter, therefore, is not only about teaching you to resist. It reveals a code. An invisible pattern behind those who fall and those who remain unshaken. A code that begins with the silence of discipline, is strengthened by the power of premeditated decision, and reaches its peak in the ability to say "no" before even hearing the invitation. Whoever waits to resist only when the proposal is made has already lost the territory of the mind. The true battlefield of temptation is not the moment of the proposal but the preparation that precedes every possible choice.

This is the call that echoes deep within every vigilant soul. Train your mind before desire speaks louder.

Strengthen your soul while there is still time. Shield your thoughts with firm decisions so that when the attack comes, the answer is already programmed. Because, in the end, the one who overcomes temptation is not the strongest. It is the one who is most prepared. Resistance is not born from the impulse of emotion, but from the silent construction of a non-negotiable identity.

EVIL ENTERS THROUGH THE CRACKS THAT ROUTINE IGNORED

The brain does not decide at the moment temptation appears. It merely executes previously installed patterns. When someone faces a moral or emotional choice, what seems like a spontaneous decision is, in reality, an automatic reaction based on mental structures already formed. If the mind has not been trained to resist, it will give in. Not because of weakness, but because of unconscious programming. Temptation does not invade a well-guarded territory. It exploits doors that have been left ajar by daily negligence.

Research conducted by Benjamin Libet showed that the brain begins a decision-making process up to seven seconds before a person becomes conscious of the choice. Later studies at Harvard University confirmed this interval, revealing that a large part of our decisions is anticipated by habits built beforehand. This completely changes our understanding of what resistance is. The true battlefield of temptation is not at the moment of the clash.

It unfolds much earlier, in the silence of routine, in the backstage of discipline, in the constant practice of saying "no" before the proposal even exists.

Genuine resistance is not born from the emotion of the moment, but from the firmness of already established convictions. It is not the strongest who win, but the most determined. Those who cultivate inner clarity, solid purposes, and values that do not change with circumstances. They do not react to chaos with despair. They were already prepared before the storm.

This preparation does not happen by chance. It is shaped in daily decisions, in the repetition of small victories that silently mold the soul. Just as an antivirus works before the system is attacked, a trained mind identifies and neutralizes temptation before it even develops. It is a lifestyle built in silence, far from applause, but which reveals itself in the moment of crisis.

This culture of readiness is studied among military forces, elite athletes, rescue teams, and high-performance environments. But it also applies to the spiritual realm. Those who cultivate their inner structure with discipline are rarely caught off guard by error. Because preparation eliminates the cracks through which temptation usually enters.

The mistake many make is relying only on willpower. Science proves that it is limited. Roy Baumeister, one of today's most respected psychologists, showed in his "ego depletion" theory that willpower behaves like a muscle.

The more you use it, the more it wears out. Therefore, those who make many decisions throughout the day or live under constant pressure become more vulnerable to giving in. Relying solely on momentary effort is leaving room for collapse. Without a lifestyle based on consistency and self-control, even the most sincere intention can be defeated by the most trivial impulse.

Resisting is not a hurried decision made in the midst of a crisis. It is a foundation built with practice, vision, and faithfulness to the truth. Those who make goodness their natural path do not need to struggle in desperation to reject evil. Because evil no longer has space. True resistance is not born from heroic acts. It is the result of daily, invisible, and faithful training that transforms future decisions into automatic reactions rooted in integrity.

In the end, it is not the strength of the moment that defines victory. It is the faithfulness of the silent days that came before. It is the sum of small, conscious, and intentional choices. Victory over temptation begins long before the invitation to sin. It begins when you consistently decide to train your mind to recognize danger and strengthen your soul to make no concessions.

EVERY PERSON'S JOURNEY IS MARKED BY TWO CHOICES: TO RESIST OR TO BE DOMINATED

AThe story of Joseph and Potiphar's wife is one of the greatest biblical demonstrations of intelligent resistance.

He did not wait for the moment of seduction to reflect. His decision was made long before the invitation. He did not step into the field of temptation to test his strength because he knew the secret was not in being stronger but in being wiser. Joseph did not face temptation with arguments. He faced it with distance. He fled. And by fleeing, he ruled. Whoever flees today will reign tomorrow. Those who see temptation as something small often face it as if they were invincible, but those who view it as a silent poison treat it with the gravity it deserves. Fleeing, in this context, is synonymous with strategic wisdom. It is not cowardice. It is preemptive self-control. It is the sharp discernment of what is at stake when you close your eyes to rationalize what should be avoided.

Daniel, in turn, presents us with a pedagogy of firmness built in the silence of routine. He did not devise survival strategies when he was thrown into the lions' den. He was already strengthened before the decree was signed. In Daniel 1:8, we read that he resolved in his heart not to defile himself. This decision preceded any threat. When the test came, his answer had already been forged in secret. In Daniel 6:10, we see that he prayed three times a day, as usual. His spiritual discipline was an invisible shield. He did not improvise faith. He cultivated conviction. This is the difference between those who react and those who resist: those who react risk giving in to the heat of the moment, but those who resist have already built their inner wall before the invasion. Daniel's firmness is living proof that spiritual consistency in times of peace is what sustains integrity in times of war.

On the other hand, Samson reveals the tragic portrait of someone who underestimates temptation. Physically strong but emotionally fragile, he believed he could toy with sin without suffering the consequences. His confidence was in his past deeds, not in his present vigilance. He got close to Delilah believing he was in control, but each time she pressed him, he surrendered another inch of his soul. He relied on his own strength and ignored the signs of spiritual weariness. When he finally revealed his secret, his strength had already been replaced by an irreversible emptiness. He rose as before, but did not know that the Spirit had already left him. Temptation did not destroy him all at once. It seduced him little by little, weakened his defenses, and, in the end, harvested the fruits of neglect. Samson is a warning to all of us: those who play with the blade will soon lack the strength to hold the sword. Temptation does not strike in a single day. It weakens you slowly until no resistance is left.

And so this contrast does not feel too distant from the modern reader, look around: Joseph's story repeats itself in young people who avoid ambiguous flirts in inboxes, who do not entertain dubious conversations, or who do not stay alone in compromising situations. Daniel's story echoes in professionals who refuse to falsify reports, even when no one is watching, because their values do not change with circumstances. And Samson's tragedy plays out, day after day, in leaders, influencers, pastors, and ordinary people who, little by little, give in to the shine of social media, the power of vanity, or the comfort of unguarded pleasure, until, before they realize it, they no longer have the strength to rise again.

> *"Every great collapse began with small cracks left unrepaired."*

HOW TO REPROGRAM THE BRAIN TO SAY "NO"

Resisting temptation is not a gift reserved for the virtuous. It is a skill that can be trained, shaped, and improved. The brain, with its incredible capacity for adaptation, responds directly to the stimuli it receives frequently. This means that resisting evil is not a matter of chance. It is a construction. It is like sharpening a sword before the war begins. Neuroscience calls this neural plasticity. What you repeat, the brain registers as a safe path. The more you say "no," the more the brain learns that this is the natural response. The small victories you achieve daily are not insignificant. They are the paving stones of a safe road when the days of trial come.

Train your mind to see beyond the moment.

This is one of the most effective keys to resistance. The technique of cognitive restructuring starts precisely here. Every temptation presents itself as an immediate pleasure but hides future consequences. Visualizing the pain behind visible pleasures is like putting a long-range lens on the now. Those who learn to see what lies behind the curtain of desire develop a kind of clarity that saves the soul before it stumbles. It is like anticipating the fall and building a bridge before the hole.

Discipline as the foundation of self-control.

Discipline sustains self-control when emotions want to take the wheel. Those who build solid habits do not live at the mercy of motivation. They do not depend on emotional climate to do what is right. They understand that great walls of protection are built with daily bricks of consistency. A single act of discipline will not solve everything, but a routine of discipline becomes a shield against impulsiveness.

The 10-minute technique.

Among practical tools, there is one that seems simple but is profoundly effective: the 10-minute technique. Instead of giving in to desire immediately, wait. Breathe. Walk. Pray. Research shows that impulses lose strength over time. The desire that screams in your ears in the first minute often barely whispers by the tenth. The impulse is not invincible; it is simply impatient. Give your mind time, and you will see that the fire dies when the wind of haste is not fanned. Desire is a lit match. And like any match, it goes out on its own if it does not find fuel.

Identity as the key to lasting resistance.

Beyond techniques, there is one factor that redefines everything: identity. Temptation finds space where identity is fractured. When someone sees themselves as weak, lacking control, or as someone who "always fails," the brain aligns decisions with that image. But when the inner vision is solid, when the person sees themselves as someone with integrity, strong, guided by principles, saying "no" becomes more natural than saying "yes." The brain always seeks coherence between what we think of ourselves and what we do. Therefore, changing the internal narrative transforms external behaviors. Those who believe they are free make decisions of freedom. Those who see themselves as prisoners, even if outside the cell, will continue to behave as if they were chained.

Victory belongs to the most prepared.

Victory over temptation does not belong to the strongest but to the most prepared. Those who train their minds before the battle win effortlessly when the war comes. Because the battlefield has already been conquered in the silence of the room, in moments of prayer, in the choice to say "no" when no one was watching. Resisting is not an emotional reaction. It is a programmed response. A defense built on ordinary days that becomes an unbreakable shield on difficult days.

Samson trusted in his strength. Joseph trusted in his flight. Samson tried to win in the field of provocation. Joseph triumphed in the field of prudence. One fell before seduction. The other rose through decision. The difference between falling and resisting lies in who you decide to be before temptation knocks at the door.

Because, in the end, evil does not destroy the strong. It destroys those who were unprepared. And every soul that chooses to win, even before the war begins, is already standing on the side of victory.

Chapter 10

THE FINAL TEST:

THE GREATEST CHALLENGE OF TEMPTATION BEFORE YOUR GREATEST VICTORY

"A runner does not feel the true weight of the race in the first kilometer, but in the final meters. A soldier does not face the fiercest attack at the start of the war, but when victory is near. The final test is not about physical resistance but about the exhaustion that undermines perseverance. Because the enemy knows that if you keep going, he loses."

The most dangerous moment of any journey is not the beginning, nor the middle. It is the end. This is the point where many give up. Not because they lack strength, but because the last phase of the battle feels like the most intense. Physical, mental, and spiritual exhaustion accumulate. Doubt settles in. The voice of giving up seems louder than ever. And the enemy, cunning as always, intensifies his attacks precisely when the finish line is closest.

Why does this happen? Because the goal of temptation is not just to divert your path. It is to make you stop right when you are about to reach your purpose. It is to weaken your faith at the exact moment when the reward is about to come. The danger of the final test lies in its disguise. It does not appear as an open attack. It wears the mask of legitimate reasons, emotional arguments, and understandable justifications. All with one single objective: to make you believe that you are fighting for something that may never happen.

This is the moment when many give up on their marriage, their calling, their mission, their dream. Not because they have failed along the way, but because they did not know how to bear the weight of "almost." When the promise is about to be fulfilled, obstacles arise that seem insurmountable, crises appear that never happened before, and the most treacherous of all, the fear that everything was in vain.

But there is a secret that few understand: if the fight feels harder than ever, it may be because victory has never been this close.

THE PSYCHOLOGY OF THE FINALOBSTACLE

If you have ever run a marathon or faced a long personal journey, you know that the greatest exhaustion does not reveal itself at the start. It settles in at the end, when the mind begins to question whether it is still worth continuing. The body may be at its limit, but it is the mind that decides whether you keep going or turn back. It is at this very moment that temptation takes its most subtle and dangerous form: not as sin, but as the urge to quit.

Science offers clear explanations. The so-called "decision fatigue" occurs when the brain is exposed to a long sequence of choices, leading to mental exhaustion. The mind, already overloaded, seeks easier escape routes. The fatigue of deciding, of maintaining focus, of fighting for so long, makes one vulnerable to giving up at the most critical moment.

Another determining factor is emotional exhaustion. The more we invest in something, the higher our expectations of the outcome. And it is precisely this accumulated expectation that makes the final stretch so painful. Internal pressure grows. Doubts multiply. And the heart, once full of faith, now feels invaded by God's silence and by the echo of unanswered questions.

But there is an even more insidious enemy: the fear of change. The human mind, even while desiring transformation, resists it. The last stage of the process does not just challenge your strength. It confronts your identity. Breaking free from the old version of yourself is frightening. Many give up not because they failed, but because they were not ready to become who they needed to be.

Scripture mirrors this reality. Abraham climbed Mount Moriah with the promise in his hands and the hardest command in his heart. He was not tested at the beginning of his journey but at the end, when everything seemed settled. Jesus, in Gethsemane, did not face only physical pain, but the weight of a choice that would redefine eternity. His greatest agony was not the cross itself, but the moment before it, where His soul groaned to the point of sweating blood. David, too, had the chance to seize the throne by force, after years of running and persecution. But he chose to wait for God's timing, resisting the temptation to rush the process.

These men had something in common: they did not retreat in the face of the final test. They understood that the pressure at the end is often the confirmation stamp that the promise is near. The despair of the end may simply be the echo of what is about to be born.

This pattern is not confined to the Bible. It appears in everyday battles. In the entrepreneur who worked for years in silence but gave up just a step away from recognition. In the woman who went through every stage of fertility treatment but stopped just before the positive result. In the young man who fought addictions for so long but thought a relapse was proof that he could never change. In the writer who abandoned the manuscript out of fear of criticism, not knowing that the book would become an answer for thousands of lives.

The enemy does not need to destroy your dreams. He only needs to convince you that they will not come true. And he will do this when you are most vulnerable. When the fight feels unbearable, when everything is more confusing than clear, when heaven seems silent and the ground unstable, that is when you must stop and reflect: could this be a sign that I am closer than ever?

HOW TO ENDURE THE FINAL TEST AND STAND FIRM UNTIL VICTORY

There are moments when heaven seems closed, the ground beneath you feels unsteady, and your soul begins to doubt even what it once firmly believed. This is not just the end of the journey. This is the territory of the final test. The point where many stumble not because they lack faith, but because the weight of "almost" is heavier than the fear of failure. The final test is treacherous because it disguises itself as logic. It comes with thoughts like, "You've already done enough," "Maybe it wasn't meant to be," "No one will judge you if you stop now."

But it is precisely in this foggy zone that great destinies are sealed. Not by emotions, but by decisions that hold firm even without any sensory encouragement. Because those who remain when everything loses meaning are not stubborn. They are forged.

The kind of resistance that matters is not loud. It is silent. It does not manifest in shouting but in persistence. It does not need an audience to exist, nor signs to continue.

Its fuel is the conviction that the promise is worth more than immediate relief.

Learn to decipher the invisible war. When opposition intensifies in unusual ways, when everything around you begins to demand immediate answers and doubts multiply, understand this: the fiercest storm comes just before the sky clears. Chaos is the dress rehearsal before the curtain rises for the new act.

The Bible is full of characters who won hidden battles before celebrating public victories. Elijah collapsed emotionally right after confronting the prophets of Baal and being used by God for one of the most powerful miracles of the Old Testament. He did not fall because he was weak. He fell because he was at the end. And it was there, in the desert of exhaustion, that God whispered the gentlest, most restorative voice of his journey. The final test is not the fall itself. It is what you do with it. True failure is not falling. It is believing that the fall is the end.

Avoid making decisions with a tired soul. Emotional exhaustion distorts perspectives, shortens horizons, and magnifies pain. Fatigue makes it seem as if the seed will never sprout, as if prayers were never heard, as if God's silence means absence when in fact it means maturation. A farmer does not abandon his field because he does not see sprouts in seven days. He trusts the timing. The faith that endures the final test is a faith that understands heaven's rhythm.

If you are tempted to stop, it may be because you are very close to crossing a spiritual threshold. The enemy does not attack with such fury those who are still far off. He focuses his efforts on those who are about to break free from an old season and step into something that threatens the gates of hell. This is why Jesus' Gethsemane is so revealing. His pain there was not just physical. It was existential. It was His soul being crushed by a decision that would change eternity. And even while sweating blood, He remained.

Perhaps your current battle is not only against circumstances, but against the old version of yourself that is trying to survive. Every great change requires burying an outdated identity. Many give up not because the journey is impossible, but because they are not ready to leave behind who they once were.

This is where the power of faithfulness comes in. Faithfulness is not about not feeling fear. It is about moving forward despite it. It is walking even without visibility. It is saying "I'm still here" even when everything inside you wants to run. Faithfulness is the language of those who endure the final test. And this is what God is looking for when He gazes upon the earth.

When everything seems to be collapsing, ask yourself: *What if this is just the final contraction before the birth of the promise? What if this pain is the sign of a new cycle? What if this silence is the exact interval between the end of one season and the breakthrough of the next?*

The final test always tries to convince you that none of this was worth it. But the truth is different: if you've made it this far, it is because something far greater is waiting on the other side. And God never wastes pain. Every tear you have shed will be counted as a seed. Every waiting period will be answered. And every sacrifice will be remembered when heaven opens over you.

Do not stop. Not now. Not this close. The story you will tell afterward will make sense of even the most confusing parts of the journey. Because those who endure the final test do not just win. They become unrecognizable. Not because they lost something along the way, but because they rose again as someone completely new.

Chapter 11

THE TEMPTATION OF STATUS:

WHEN THE DESIRE TO BE IMPORTANT CORRUPTS YOUR ESSENCE

"The pursuit of status doesn't destroy all at once; it erodes slowly. First, it turns convictions into concessions. Then, it transforms authenticity into a character you perform. And before you realize it, you are no longer the owner of yourself but a hostage to the need of being seen. The worst temptation is not losing what you have but giving up who you are to maintain an illusion. How many have sacrificed their values in exchange for a pedestal?"

In Eden, the serpent did not promise a fruit. It promised a status. *"You will be like God"* (Genesis 3:5). Since then, humanity has confused identity with image, and calling with visibility. The temptation of status does not corrupt immediately; it seduces through vanity, paving the path with compliments, until one no longer walks by calling but by the need to be acclaimed.

The downfall of Judas began when he grew frustrated with the messianic silence of Jesus. He expected a king to overthrow Rome, not a servant who would wash feet. Craig Keener points out that Judas may have tried to force Jesus to manifest Himself as a political leader. But by attempting to rush the throne, he accelerated the cross. His betrayal was not merely for coins but for the craving of a prominence that heaven never promised him.

Saul, anointed to reign, forgot that a throne without submission to heaven becomes a snare. He governed with his eyes on the people and his back to God. The moment he prioritized popular applause, he lost the anointing that sustained him. He did not fall because of weakness, but because of vanity. He didn't lose the crown to external enemies, but through internal alliances with the idolatry of acceptance.

And the Pharisees? They were devoted to performance. They no longer served God. They served the mirror of religion. They traded intimacy for recognition and the altar for theater. Jesus exposed them with words that still echo today: *"You love the places of honor... you like to*

be called teachers... but inside you are full of bones and rot"
(Matthew 23:6-27, paraphrased).

Status is a refined temptation because it appeals to
the best of humanity: its ability to inspire. But when it
disconnects from character and anchors itself in appearance, what was once a calling turns into a show. Leadership loses its sense of service, and mission becomes a stage.
The ego starts dictating the route, and the heart no longer
knows how to be authentic. It's like living chained to the
opinions of others, smiling on the outside while dying on
the inside. What is most tragic is that many don't even
realize they are imprisoned. Living to be noticed is the
first step to no longer living truly.

THE ILLUSION OF STATUS: WHEN SUCCESS
BECOMES A PRISON

Recognition is one of temptation's subtlest weapons.
It does not come as opposition but as reward. It presents
itself elegantly, disguised as honor, opportunities, and
sincere applause. At first, everything seems legitimate. After all, there is nobility in being valued for what is done
with excellence. But the danger reveals itself when praise
begins to corrode the roots of conviction, and the desire
for applause overshadows the hunger for God's presence.
What was once a vocation becomes a showcase. What
was once an altar becomes a stage.

Neuroscience sheds light on this process with disconcerting precision. Dopamine, the neurotransmitter of pleasure and reward, is strongly activated by social acceptance—likes, compliments, invitations, numbers. Each of these triggers pleasure centers in the brain, creating a subtle yet corrosive dependency. And like any dependency, it requires growing doses. Yesterday's praise no longer satisfies today. The soul, which should be guided by principles, begins to feed on the next validation.

The desire to be seen is not inherently wrong. But when the need for recognition suffocates commitment to faithfulness, success becomes a prison. What should have been a steppingstone for service turns into a throne for self-preservation. And in this process, many lose their essence on the path of ascension.

External validation is an exhausting cycle. The standard that once elevated now imprisons. The image must be maintained, and the smallest misstep is interpreted as a downfall. One lives as a servant to an invisible audience, hostage to emotional algorithms, trapped in a persona that must be performed daily. And the cruelest part: over time, the person playing the role forgets who they were before the act began.

The cost of self-promotion is not paid in money. It is paid in sleepless nights, undiagnosed anxiety, and fatigue that no rest can cure. Many are not tired from the demands of work but from the burden of maintaining an image that no longer represents who they are. Status is costly. It demands continuous performance. And prolonged performance kills authenticity.

The fear of losing one's place corrupts decisions. Pastors avoid uncomfortable truths to keep their audience. Artists soften their essence to please trends. Professionals remain silent in the face of injustice to protect connections. The idolatry of status silences prophets, drains courage, and anesthetizes integrity.

Status, in essence, is not the enemy. It becomes dangerous when it takes the throne of the heart. When what you have begins to define who you are. When external shine overshadows internal truth. When reputation becomes more valuable than authenticity. In this scenario, "seeming" overshadows "being," and calling gives way to convenience.

Influence is a tool. But when it becomes the goal, it loses its sanctity. Recognition that does not stem from faithfulness is a sweet poison: it praises while it weakens, elevates while it manipulates, applauds while it disfigures.

Scripture does not hide the tragedy of those who succumbed to the final test. In the final stretch, where God's glory draws near, many stumbled not because of obvious weakness but because of subtle desires that seemed justified. This is the test of "almost," of being on the verge of being crowned, of being on the brink of breakthrough but falling for trusting too much in oneself or for desiring too much of what the ego projected.

Saul is the bitter portrait of one who fails in the final meters. When the wait for the prophet Samuel was extended, he could not endure the pressure of silence and decided to act on his own. The fear of man's judgment spoke louder than obedience to God's command. His mistake was not just the act of sacrifice, but anxiety disguised as zeal. He lost the anointing long before he lost the crown. Because God rejects those who prefer to appear spiritual rather than truly obey.

The Pharisees, masters of appearance, were consumed by the temptation of prestige. They did not fall into visible moral sin but into the subtlest trap: vanity dressed as devotion. Jesus denounced them with cutting words. They were whitewashed tombs, beautiful on the outside but dead inside. They loved the spotlight of the temple but despised the God of the temple. They were revered by men but unknown by God.

Judas, like a living parable, reveals that the final test is not always about resisting evil, but about enduring the frustration of an unmet plan. His fall was not driven only by greed. It was by creating a Messiah in his own image. He expected political glory, national revenge, Caesar's throne. But he saw Jesus take the path of the cross. And unable to accept a purpose that did not meet his own dreams, he sold eternity for thirty pieces of silver. His betrayal was not the start of his fall. It was the outcome of a misplaced expectation.

Status seduces because it speaks the language of the ego. It offers a golden promise of importance, influence, and approval. But what begins as honor can turn into disguised idolatry. And the scariest part is that crossing that line happens in silence. No one notices when one stops serving God and starts building for themselves.

This is why the final test demands discernment. Strength is not enough. Awareness is needed. The question is never just "What am I doing?" but "Why am I doing it?" Am I building for God or for my image? Am I fulfilling a calling or promoting an ambition? Without this inner examination, the final stretch can deceive us with applause, stages, and titles that look like achievements but are traps for a heart led astray.

The temptation of status is not defeated by running away but by being deeply rooted. Only those whose identity is grounded in God can walk through applause without getting lost in the noise. Humility is not the opposite of greatness. It is the invisible foundation that sustains those who reach the end without being corrupted.

HOW TO LIVE WITH PURPOSE WITHOUT BECOMING A PRISONER OF OTHER PEOPLE'S OPINIONS

True greatness is not measured by how many follow you, but by how firm you stand when no one is watching. The stage reveals talent, but the desert reveals character. Public glory without private foundation is like a sandcastle: impressive from afar, but it crumbles at the slightest touch of truth. Real greatness blossoms in the solitude of unseen decisions, in the choices no one witnesses but that shape everything you will be when the lights go out.

It is not about building an image, but sustaining an identity. Image can be molded, edited, masked, manipulated. Identity is root. It is what remains when masks fall. It is the name heaven knows, not the one algorithms promote. There are those who live for the eyes of men and lose sight of themselves. There are those who shine so much on the outside that they extinguish the light within. The question that echoes deep in the soul is not "Who admires you?" but "Who are you when no one is watching anymore?"

Differentiate identity from image. Image is a reflection. Identity is essence. Image can be altered by filters, angles, and narratives. Identity is that silent rock that does not change with the wind. Image can make you influential. Identity makes you integral. And when image becomes more important than identity, the soul begins to wither. Because it exists not to be, but to appear to be. What is built only to impress can become a prison disguised as a palace. And the more one lives to maintain an image, the more one forgets who they truly are.

Develop confidence that does not depend on an audience. True security is born when you remain faithful to your purpose even on cloudy days, when no one recognizes or applauds you. It is in that silence that heaven speaks louder. The heart at peace with God does not need likes to validate its existence. Those who walk with inner clarity carry a courage that is not noisy but unshakable. Because they do not move to be noticed, but because they were commissioned.

Practice humility as a shield against the vanity of status. Humility is not about diminishing yourself; it is about remembering where you came from and who lifted you up. There is no shame in being behind the scenes if that is where God is shaping you. The stage may offer visibility, but only the backstage offers maturity. A true leader is not one who demands honor, but one who serves with love. Because those who serve out of conviction will never be enslaved by the need to be served out of vanity.

Status is a seductive idol because it offers power without purpose. It seduces with promises of greatness but charges with emptiness. It is a ladder that pushes you to the top but has no roots in the ground of integrity. And those who climb without moral foundations end up falling from the height of their own illusions. When the soul depends on applause for peace, silence becomes torture. Status can give position, but only purpose gives direction. And without direction, even success is an abyss in disguise.

Before you desire to be noticed, desire to be whole. Because integrity is worth more than visibility. Before wanting to echo, seek to have roots. Before speaking to crowds, have the courage to speak truth to yourself. Before gaining influence, build coherence. And before stepping onto a stage, make sure you still have an altar.

Heaven does not reward performance. It rewards faithfulness. It is not about how much you impress, but how much you endure.

If your worth depends on others, you have never truly owned yourself. You have been a tenant of other people's expectations. And no one is free as long as they need approval to exist. True freedom is born when you trade the need for acceptance for the courage to be real. When you no longer live to please, but to fulfill. Because those who live to fulfill their calling do not fear the silence of criticism, nor are they intoxicated by the sound of applause. They know heaven has already approved them, and that is enough.

HOW TO REVERSE THE DAMAGE OF TEMPTATION:

IS THERE A WAY BACK?

"Temptation may have knocked you down, but it only wins if it convinces you not to get up. Mistakes are not the end. They are commas in the story. What defines your destiny is not the fall, but the choice to continue. There is always a way back, and the only true defeat is believing that there is no more hope."

Temptation may have won a battle, but the war is far from over.

The greatest problem is rarely the mistake itself. The most effective strategy of temptation is not simply to make you fall. It is to keep you lying down. The ground, which should be a place of impact, becomes a prison when you accept that you no longer have the right to start again. The enemy's greatest trick is not in the act of seduction but in the power of accusation. He does not need to keep you sinning if he can keep you silent, far from God's presence, locked in guilt.

Guilt keeps the soul chained to yesterday. Shame isolates the heart in the present. And when repentance is misinterpreted, it turns into a paralyzing weight. The soul begins to ask itself the same question as if it were a final sentence: *Is there still a way back?*

If mistakes were the final point of the narrative, David would have vanished from history after adultery and murder. Peter would have been erased from the mission after denying Jesus. Paul, once a ruthless persecutor, would never have written the letters that shaped Christian thought for centuries. But all these men experienced the touch of a God who does not cancel lives because of failures, but rewrites them with the ink of grace.

Jesus did not leave Peter imprisoned by the bitter taste of betrayal. He sought him out. Restored his dignity. Rekindled his mission. Peter failed publicly, but he was restored in intimacy. And after that, he was not left on the sidelines. He was reinstated to the front lines. His failure did not silence him. On the contrary, it made his voice more human, more aware of the grace that sustained him.

The real question is not if you fell. The question is: do you still have the courage to rise again?

WHY DO SO MANY PEOPLE GIVE UP AFTER THEY FALL?

Temptation rarely strikes with full force. It is subtle, progressive, and silent. It operates in two phases, like a cycle of spiritual manipulation. First, it whispers that giving in will bring no consequences, that no one needs to know, that it is just this one time. But after the fall, the voice changes tone. The whisper turns into a shout. It stops persuading and starts accusing. The same voice that said it would not matter now screams condemnation. It pushes you into the mistake and then uses the mistake to keep you from seeking restoration. It is an emotional prison that begins with seduction and ends with a sentence.

And the result of this prison is devastating. Many people do not drift away from God because they sinned, but because they believe their sin has canceled any possibility of return. It is not the mistake that kills them inside. It is the belief that the mistake was the end of the road. What should have been a temporary detour becomes a permanent route away from God's presence. Pain becomes identity. Guilt builds walls so high that repentance can no longer climb. And the repentant soul begins to believe that grace is for the strong, not for those who have fallen again.

Guilt paralyzes. It does not just weigh. It suffocates. Instead of generating repentance, it becomes a chain on the shoulders, a constant reminder that the person has failed and therefore does not deserve to go on. Many abandon their faith not because they stopped loving God, but because they believe God has stopped loving them. Not due to a lack of faith, but because of an excess of accusation. Guilt contaminates identity until the repentant soul feels unworthy even to try to rise again.

Shame redefines identity. It robs you of the right to say "I made a mistake," and replaces it with "I am the mistake." What should have been a turbulent chapter becomes the title of the entire story. And when identity is corrupted, behavior follows. A person begins to live at the level of the shame they believe they carry. The fall becomes the mirror, the new name, the new narrative. Pain is no longer an event. It becomes the place where the soul decides to live.

The fear of judgment silences. It is not the sin that terrifies the most. It is the possibility of being discovered. Many stay silent not because they want to, but because they are afraid. Afraid of being exposed, judged, rejected. Afraid of harsh looks and cutting words. So they choose the anonymity of pain over the exposure that could bring healing. Forced smiles become shields. Disappearance becomes refuge. Shame becomes a hiding place. They would rather carry the burden alone than risk being shamed before others, even though only the light can heal what the darkness hides.

But there is an essential and transforming difference between guilt and repentance. Guilt paralyzes. Repentance mobilizes. Guilt looks at the mistake as ruin. Repentance sees it as a foundation for rebuilding. Guilt says "It is too late." Repentance says "It starts here." Guilt points to the failure. Repentance points to the Father. Guilt distances you. Repentance reconnects you. The enemy uses guilt to keep you on the ground. God uses repentance to lift you up and take you farther than before.

A mistake can leave a scar, but it does not have to be a sentence. It can become the mark of a battle won, not a war lost. The Bible does not hide the falls of its heroes. It shows them with honesty because every fall became the stage for even greater grace.

David and Bathsheba: The mistake that did not define his destiny (2 Samuel 11, Psalm 51).

David did not just stumble into temptation. He planned it, gave in to it, abused the power he held, and then tried to cover it with blood what began with desire. David's sin was not circumstantial. It was progressive. An adultery followed by a murder. By human standards, the verdict would have been final. Cancellation, shame, end of the story. But David's story reminds us that the depth of a mistake is never greater than the depth of grace.

Psalm 51 was not written in a temple or before an audience. It was written on the ground of guilt, watered by the tears of a king stripped of glory and confronted by his own conscience. There is no performance in his words, only a soul laid bare before God. He did not just ask for forgiveness. He asked for a new heart. David did not seek to erase the past, but to transform the future. He preferred to lose the crown rather than live a day without the presence of the Spirit.

The world would have buried David in the same grave where many have been buried by their failures. But God looked at his heart, not his record. The man who fell before the eyes of a nation was the same man who wrote that God will never despise a broken heart. It was not the mistake that defined David, but the repentance that rebuilt him. His story still echoes because heaven does not end promises based on bad chapters.

Peter and the Denial of Jesus: The Pain of the Fall and the Power of Restoration

Peter did not fail out of ignorance. He failed with full awareness. The one who had walked on water and promised eternal loyalty was the same one who denied knowing Jesus publicly, and he did it three times. His fall was quick, painful, and humiliating. The rooster crowed, and with it came the collapse of Peter's entire image of himself. It was not just a slip. It was a brutal encounter with his own fragility.

But the gospel does not end with the rooster. It restarts with the embers of forgiveness. When Jesus rose again, He did not avoid Peter, nor did He accuse him. He called him closer. Not to humiliate him, but to restore him. The scene at the lake is more than symbolic. It is surgical. Three denials healed with three questions, each one piercing deeper than the last. There are no long speeches, just a repeated question that reaches the exact point of the wound.

Jesus was not interested in punishment but in restoration. He knew that the pain of the fall could become the foundation of a stronger mission. Peter was not only forgiven. He was re-sent. The same mouth that had denied Jesus was commissioned to preach. The public failure was compensated with a personal calling. This shows us that Christ's forgiveness is never just emotional. It is functional. He heals to re-send. He restores to rewrite the story.

The Prodigal Son: Coming Home and the Grace Without Conditions

The prodigal son did not simply ask for his inheritance early. He symbolically declared that his father was dead to him. He left in haste, lived as if there were no tomorrow, squandered everything he had, and ended up in a pigsty. But the lowest point was not hunger or misery. It was the idea that he would never again be worthy of being called a son. What broke him was not the lack of bread, but the lack of belonging.

With a rehearsed speech full of guilt and submission, he decided to return. Not with the expectation of a party, but with fear of rejection. However, before he could finish his confession, he was interrupted by an embrace. A father who ran to meet him. Who did not ask for proof or timelines for change. Who did not mention losses or expose shame. He simply called for a feast.

The sandals, the ring, and the robe were not just gifts. They were visible declarations that his identity was intact. Restoration began before repentance ended. Because the father's love did not wait for change. He anticipated it with grace. The son did not return to be a servant. He returned to be a son again. And the house he thought he had lost was still in the same place, waiting not for a perfect apology, but for a determined return.

The greatest power of the parable lies in the scandal of grace. There are no merits. No negotiations. Only a love that refuses to let the fall be the final point.

THE NEUROSCIENCE OF REPENTANCE AND CHANGE

The human brain was not designed to live chained to the past. Though memories can weigh us down, its deepest structure is built for movement, reinvention, and hope. Inside us lives one of the most extraordinary structures of the known universe, created with the ability to learn, unlearn, and relearn. The human mind carries the gift of reorganizing itself after traumas, falls, and moral failures. We call this ability neuroplasticity. What is most fascinating is that this science is not locked in laboratories or reserved for an intellectual elite. It is available to everyone who refuses to die where they have fallen.

Mistakes have never been the final sentence of life. What truly shapes someone's journey is not the mistake made, but the decision taken right after the fall. Redemption begins when the heart refuses to accept the fall as a permanent identity.

The plasticity of the brain and the reprogramming of harmful patterns. Psychiatrist Norman Doidge, in his book *The Brain That Changes Itself*, describes the brain as a field where mental paths are formed through constant repetition. If harmful habits can be learned, they can also be unlearned. Imagine a snow-covered field. Every time you walk in the same spot, that path becomes automatic and deep. But if, with intention, you step in a different direction, even if it feels uncertain, new paths begin to form. Repentance works the same way. It is not just a moral chill or an emotional weight. It is an active, daily decision that, when practiced, literally changes the brain's chemistry and opens new pathways of behavior.

The same brain that memorized lies can be trained to sustain truth. The mind that once gave in to impulsiveness can be taught self-control. This is not an overnight miracle. It is an intentional process. And like every true process, it requires consistency, focus, and faith.

How the mind processes repentance and the search for redemption. Studies in affective neuroscience reveal that genuine repentance activates deep regions like the prefrontal cortex and the limbic system. These areas are directly linked to decision-making, empathy, and the sense of moral value. When a person sincerely recognizes their mistake and seeks transformation, they do not just feel guilt; they cognitively register the impact of that failure. The brain begins to associate the mistake with the emotional pain it caused and naturally builds a barrier against repeating that behavior.

This is why true repentance is not reduced to tears or laments. It is an act of neural re-education. It is a silent, effective reconstruction of how we feel, react, and choose. In both scientific and spiritual terms, repentance is a bridge between pain and change. It is the beginning of a new narrative. It is not the end of the road, but the beginning of redemption.

The importance of time and patience in the rebuilding process. No soul rebuilds itself overnight. Not even the most powerful brain can reconfigure itself by decree. Neuroscience confirms that lasting changes are born from consistency. Every new correct decision strengthens healthy neural connections. Every choice aligned with truth reinforces the restored circuits that sustain a new identity. This is how old patterns dissolve, and the new ones solidify.

In this process, patience is not an accessory but the foundation. It is not about speed. It is about depth. The impatient seek immediate results. The wise understand that roots take time to grow strong. Visible growth is only a reflection of what has already been established in the invisible layers of the being. Every perseverant action becomes the cement for rebuilding an integral mind.

Just like a fractured bone, when treated with precision and care, returns stronger, the mind can become more resilient after a fall. What was once fertile ground for error can be turned into holy ground for integrity. Guilt may wound, but repentance heals. Science now confirms what grace has proclaimed from the beginning: starting over is possible. Restoration is achievable. And change, even when slow, will always be the most powerful testimony that no one needs to end life where they once fell.

HOW TO REBUILD YOUR LIFE AFTER FALLING INTO TEMPTATION

Restoration is not a sudden event. It is a silent process built step by step, brick by brick, soul by soul. God does not work in haste. He works with purpose. Where men look for shortcuts, heaven insists on foundations. When someone chooses to rise again, heaven does not demand speed. It demands truth. And truth has the power to pave the way back for those who have stumbled. Not with excuses wrapped in repentance, but with concrete decisions that testify to transformation. No restoration happens with feet still trapped in self-pity. No new beginning grows in soil soaked with old justifications. Whoever wants to return must walk a path made of new choices, not old laments.

Accept the reality of the mistake without living chained to guilt. Facing the truth is not about dying from it. It is about being reborn through it. The first step is not emotional. It is rational. It is looking at what happened and having the courage to say that it was real. Denying the mistake only perpetuates the wound. Running from it invites repetition. Facing it is like tearing the veil of the soul and letting light in. Recognizing the mistake is not being condemned by it. It is breaking free from the cycle that created it. Guilt imprisons because it repeats the scream of failure. Responsibility sets free because it points to maturity. God's forgiveness is not an eraser that removes pain. It is a redirection that transforms pain into purpose. When you place your fall into the right hands, it stops being shame and becomes the foundation of wisdom. Condemnation whispers that you will never be the same again. Grace responds that you will never be the same, because now you know the way back.

Identify what led to the fall so you do not repeat the same path. Repentance that does not produce change is just guilt dressed as remorse. Heaven is not impressed with tears. It responds to decisions. It is necessary to close the breaches with clarity. The human heart does not fall by accident. It slips through patterns that were ignored. Temptation is the final step of a process that began long before, when the wrong voices were heard and the right warnings were ignored. Starting over requires self-awareness. It requires the courage to review paths, detect patterns, recognize environments that seduce, and silences that scream. Starting over is not about running from the abyss. It is about building a new path where the abyss has no voice. True repentance maps out your mistakes as someone inspecting a fortress about to be rebuilt. Only those who recognize temptation before being seduced by it will win. And only those who have the courage to understand where it came from will recognize it.

Rebuild trust with yourself and with others. There is no healing without reconnection. But no reconnection happens based on words inflated by emotion. Broken trust is rebuilt with actions that are repeated over time. Every consistent gesture is a nail driven into the structure of the new bridge. Time is not the enemy of restoration. It is its greatest ally. Rushed promises create fragile expectations. Silent perseverance builds unshakable trust. Rebuilding means walking with consistency even when no one is watching. It means persisting even when no one is applauding. It means proving with actions what words can no longer justify. And above all, it means believing that the God who saw your fall is the same God who guides your restart. He does not cancel purposes because of failures. But He only rehabilitates those who accept becoming disciples on the path of reconstruction. If there is still breath, there is a chance. If there is still faith, there is a future. If there is still humility, there is healing.

Shame wants to bury what God wants to resurrect. Grace not only forgives. It lifts. It rewrites. It transforms ruins into foundations and scars into signs of redemption. Starting over with God is never a step backward. It is always a birth toward the best chapter of the story.

THE ENDGAME:

NEVER BE DECEIVED BY TEMPTATION AGAIN

"Temptation does not disappear with time. But you can become someone it can never deceive again. An experienced player does not fear the game; he understands the rules. Temptation will always return, but now you already know the patterns, the dangerous shortcuts, and the mechanisms that make so many people fall. The question is not whether temptation will return. The question is: will you continue reacting the same way?"

Temptation never arrives as a declared enemy. It hides between the lines of daily choices, in moments of exhaustion, in small concessions that seem harmless. It disguises itself as relief, as well-deserved rest, as a quick fix. It is patient. It knows how to wait for the moment when your guard is down. That is why now, after everything you have read, only one question remains. What will you do with this knowledge?

You can close this book and continue living as before. You can keep believing that it is enough to be strong when the moment comes. You can insist on trusting that your willpower will be sufficient when the situation demands a quick response. Or you can decide that this is the marker of a definitive change. From here on, there is no longer room for naivety.

What happens from this point forward does not depend on what has been written in these pages but on what you decide to do with it. Temptation is not an isolated obstacle. It is a cycle. It repeats itself with surgical precision, testing the same weaknesses, exploiting the same vulnerable points you have not yet chosen to protect.

Those who fall repeatedly believe it is enough to want to resist. But those who win understand that resistance does not begin at the moment of the fight. It begins in the silence of the backstage. In the habits that strengthen the mind long before temptation shows up. Victory is carved in the daily preparation.

True strength is not in impulsive responses. It is in building a new pattern of thought. The winner is not the strongest but the wisest. The one who understands the game before being manipulated by it. The one who recognizes the old tricks and is no longer impressed by the shiny wrapping of an old poison.

Temptation cannot control the one who chooses to cut the problem at the root. Because those who identify the cycle anticipate the blow. Those who understand the strategy no longer enter the battlefield blindly. And those who prepare with wisdom learn that the game only ends when they refuse to play by the same terms.

What will make you a winner is not a single moment of victory but the decision to live differently.

YOUR LIFE IS A CALLING, NOT A DISTRACTION

You were not born to live at the mercy of impulses. You were born to fulfill an eternal purpose. Every line you have read so far was not written just to warn you but to awaken you. Temptation is not an isolated mistake. It is a subtle strategy to take you off course. It is the detour that seems safe, the shortcut that looks smart, but in the end, it leads you far from the path God has planned for you.

Understand this clearly. Temptation is a disguised distraction. And every distraction comes with a high price. It does not steal everything at once. It slowly erodes your sense of urgency, lulls your focus to sleep, and suffocates your calling with the invisible weight of accepted concessions. It does not shout. It whispers. And what seems harmless today may be the reason for tomorrow's stagnation. Distractions are never neutral. They always compete with what matters most.

The choice is now before you. You can continue reliving the same cycles, orbiting the same dilemmas, and hoping that by some miracle the circumstances will change. Or you can decide to stand up, break the script of repetition, shatter inherited patterns, and redesign your path in the light of purpose. Nothing changes until you change. And no change is lasting without awareness of your calling.

Every yes you say to what is right strengthens your soul like a muscle being trained. Every no you offer to temptation builds an internal wall that does not shake with passing winds. What you feed within you grows like a root seeking depth. What you ignore dies from lack of space. Small, silent deviations open cracks that later turn into thunderous falls. But small correct choices, made in the anonymity of everyday life, pave the road to a life that no one can tear down.

You no longer need to fight against internal temptations if they no longer find a home in your heart. You no longer need to battle external giants when you have already conquered mastery over your own inner world. True victory begins when temptation no longer resonates with your identity.

If you look back with honesty, you will see that the greatest falls did not happen suddenly. They were built through small concessions that seemed harmless. And if you look forward with discernment, you will see that the greatest victories will be born in the hidden ground of daily decisions. It is there that destiny is shaped. It is there that purpose is strengthened. Not in great public victories, but in the silent faithfulness of each choice made in secret.

WEAPONS TO NEVER BE DECEIVED BY TEMPTATION AGAIN

VYou already understand the game. Now you need the right weapons to never be manipulated by it again. Temptation does not send an invitation. It disguises itself as opportunity, hides in haste, whispers in exhaustion, and wears the mask of necessity. That is why it is not enough to react when it arrives. You must be armed before the battle. Prepared not just with words but with rooted principles. Whoever waits for war to arm themselves has already lost the first battle.

Renewal of the mind. Romans 12:2 urges us not to conform to this world but to be transformed by the renewing of our minds. The mind is not just a stage for thoughts but the seat of spiritual decisions. It is there that it is determined whether temptation will be defeated or embraced. Those who secretly desire sin are already spiritually surrendered, even if they appear firm outwardly.

True transformation does not begin with a moral decision but with a deep change of mindset. When the mind is converted, the body follows. When you declare internally that this path no longer represents you, temptation loses its appeal. Because a renewed mind sees the eternal cost hidden behind temporary pleasures.

A converted mind is like a purified altar. It no longer accommodates strange thoughts because everything that enters is examined under the light of the cross. The Holy Spirit not only dwells in the converted heart but illuminates the mental paths that were once dark. The mind that has passed through the fire of renewal no longer seeks shortcuts. It desires truth, even when it costs something. Because it knows that those who think like Christ act like Christ.

The mental armor. Ephesians 6:10-17 reveals that resistance is not built in the heat of battle but in times of vigilance. The armor of God is not a light metaphor. It is a call to constant spiritual readiness. Those who rise without the belt of truth are exposed to lies. Those who walk without the shield of faith are vulnerable to the flaming arrows of doubt. Those who ignore the helmet of salvation risk fighting without knowing who they are in Christ. Moral and spiritual boundaries are not set in the heat of temptation. They are established in secret, in the closed room, in the days without an audience. A Christian who puts on the armor daily will not be caught off guard by the attack. A guarded mind anticipates the response. It has already decided before the test. It has already said no before the proposal arrives.

Spiritual armor is not put on with hands but with a decision of the soul. Each piece is a choice. The belt of truth demands a commitment to integrity. The breastplate of righteousness demands consistency between speech and practice. The shield of faith demands trust in the absence of evidence. The helmet of salvation demands awareness of eternal identity. And the sword of the Spirit demands intimacy with the Word. A mind covered with these truths becomes a battlefield where the enemy finds no fertile ground.

The path of wisdom. Proverbs 4:23 declares with surgical precision that from the heart flow the springs of life. And it is precisely for this reason that it must be guarded above all else. Temptation does not invade. It probes. It touches gently and hides in suggestions that seem harmless. A random thought. A feeling without filter. An acceptable justification. And when it finds fertile ground, it grows like a weed in unprotected soil. Wisdom does not just avoid sin. It avoids the environment that favors sin. A wise person does not negotiate with suggestion. They close the breaches before temptation discovers where to strike. You may not be able to prevent desire from arising, but you can decide not to feed it. Temptation does not steal what is protected. It only exploits what has been neglected. Wisdom transforms the heart into hostile territory for sin.

Fasting. Matthew 4 shows Jesus facing temptation in the desert after forty days of fasting. He did not defeat the devil by chance. He won because He was spiritually strengthened, even though He was physically weak. Fasting is not penance. It is a strategic discipline. It does not change God. It changes you. Those who learn to say no to bread discover they can say no to forbidden desires. Those who subdue small appetites are better prepared to resist great seductions. If you do not master your hunger, it will master you. Fasting weakens the flesh so that the voice of the spirit grows stronger. It is not empty deprivation but sacred training. A kind of spiritual rehearsal where you learn to silence the screams of urgency to hear the whispers of eternity. Those who fast do not just resist. They feed the inner strength that leaves temptation starving. It may knock at the door, but it dies of hunger because it no longer finds someone to feed it.

Fasting is visible renunciation that sustains invisible victories. It reconnects you to your real source. It shows you that earthly bread may sustain the body, but it does not nourish the soul. By fasting, you are not only saying no to food. You are saying yes to the dominion of the spirit over the flesh. You enter an environment where spiritual sensitivity is refined, where heaven speaks louder, and the flesh loses authority. Fasting not only prepares you for battle. It seals the heart with the authority of one who has already won within before being tested from without.

THE DECISION IS YOURS

You have walked through pages that were more than words. They were revelations, strategies, and warnings. Each chapter was a key placed in your hands. Each principle, a silent weapon against what once held you captive. Now, everything comes down to a choice.

You can close this book and continue exactly as you are. You can return to the routine that for years has disguised the emptiness. You can wait for strength to appear only on the day of battle. Or you can recognize that this is the exact moment when the cycle is broken.

You can keep hoping that one day you will resist. Or you can start building resistance today. You can keep praying like someone who repeats a request without taking action. Or you can transform your prayer into a lifestyle, where each decision is intercession in motion. You can insist on the same mistakes, stumbling on the same old ground. Or you can choose, once and for all, to change the ground you walk on.

Temptation will not stop whispering. But now you already know how to silence those voices. You have learned where it enters, how it disguises itself, and at which point it gains strength. You are no longer the same. And because of that, you can no longer pretend you do not know.

Victory over temptation is not a random miracle that falls from the sky. It is the direct result of a lifestyle that decided to align with the truth. It is the reflection of a soul that chooses vigilance when sleeping would be easier.

Preparation when procrastination would be easier. Obedience when giving in would be easier. Winning is not an event. It is a lifestyle.

The Bible never romanticized the battle. It warns. It teaches. It exposes. The devil does not need wide-open doors. A crack is enough. A slip. A well-crafted argument. With this, he plants confusion, sows fear, and destroys what took years to build. He is never in a hurry to bring you down. He only needs to distract you a little each day, wear down your faith slowly, and negotiate your truth inch by inch.

But those who have understood the rules of this game will never be fooled by it again.

You were not born to live in cycles of falling. You were called to walk in ascending cycles. Growth that, although silent to others, is visible in the spirit. You were not designed to merely survive temptation. You were empowered to master it.

And if you have made it this far, it is because something in you has already awakened. A new flame has been lit. A new version has begun to emerge. The old you, the one who justified everything with pious phrases and tolerated internal prisons disguised as freedom, is being left behind.

Let this book not be just another reading among so many. Let it be the breaking point. The beginning of a life where truth is not just read but lived. Where each page becomes like a sword sheathed in your mind. Where each revelation becomes a wall in your heart.

And when, do not ask if, but when temptation returns, because it will return, it will find someone who is no longer available to fall. Someone trained in truth, refined by pain, and forged in discipline.

May the next battle find you more prepared than ever. And may this preparation have begun today.

Not because you have become strong, but because you have decided never to be weak again.

This is not the end of the story. It is only the end of your old version.

The rest of the journey will be written by someone who has chosen to win.

Until the next battle.

BIBLIOGRAPHY

BIBLICAL AND THEOLOGICAL REFERENCES

BIBLE. Holy Bible. Various translations used, including Almeida Revista e Atualizada (ARA), New International Version (NIV), and King James Version (KJV).

KELLER, Timothy. Counterfeit Gods: The Empty Promises of Money, Sex, and Power, and the Only Hope that Matters.New York: Dutton, 2009.

LEWIS, C. S. The Screwtape Letters. New York: HarperOne, 2015.

PIPER, John. Don't Waste Your Life. Wheaton: Crossway, 2003.

BEVERE, John. The Bait of Satan: Living Free from the Deadly Trap of Offense. Lake Mary: Charisma House, 2004.

GROESCHEL, Craig. Fight: Winning the Battles That Matter Most. Grand Rapids: Zondervan, 2013.

NEUROSCIENCE AND BEHAVIORAL PSYCHOLOGY REFERENCES

BAUMEISTER, Roy; TIERNEY, John. Willpower: Rediscovering the Greatest Human Strength. New York: Penguin Press, 2011.

DUHIGG, Charles. The Power of Habit: Why We Do What We Do in Life and Business. New York: Random House, 2012.

KAHNEMAN, Daniel. Thinking, Fast and Slow. New York: Farrar, Straus and Giroux, 2011.

MCGONIGAL, Kelly. The Willpower Instinct: How Self-Control Works, Why It Matters, and What You Can Do to Get More of It. New York: Avery, 2011.

GIRARD, René. The Scapegoat. Baltimore: The Johns Hopkins University Press, 1986.

DIGITAL CULTURE, RESILIENCE, AND APPLIED PSYCHOLOGY

CIALDINI, Robert B. Influence: The Psychology of Persuasion. New York: Harper Business, 2006.

GLADWELL, Malcolm. The Tipping Point: How Little Things Can Make a Big Difference. New York: Little, Brown and Company, 2000.

NEWPORT, Cal. Digital Minimalism: Choosing a Focused Life in a Noisy World. New York: Portfolio, 2019.

HOLLIS, Rachel. Girl, Stop Apologizing. New York: HarperCollins Leadership, 2019.

www.ingramcontent.com/pod-product-compliance
Lightning Source LLC
Chambersburg PA
CBHW051525120626
46551CB00012B/1083